D0014866

Tragedy and Farce

How the American Media Sell Wars, Spin Elections, and Destroy Democracy

John Nichols and Robert W. McChesney

With illustrations by Tom Tomorrow

WITHDRAWN

CONTRA COSTA COUNTY LIBRARY

THE NEW PRESS

NEW YORK
LONDON

3 1901 03926 2961

© 2005 by John Nichols and Robert W. McChesney
Foreword © 2005 by Tim Robbins
All rights reserved.
No part of this book may be reproduced, in any form,
without written permission from the publisher.

Requests for permission to reproduce selections from this book should be mailed to:
Permissions Department, The New Press, 38 Greene Street, New York, NY 10013

Published in the United States by The New Press, New York, 2005
Distributed by W. W. Norton & Company, Inc., New York

ISBN 1-59558-016-6 (hc)
CIP data available

The New Press was established in 1990 as a not-for-profit alternative to the large, commercial publishing houses currently dominating the book publishing industry. The New Press operates in the public interest rather than for private gain, and is committed to publishing, in innovative ways, works of educational, cultural, and community value that are often deemed insufficiently profitable.

www.thenewpress.com

Composition by dix!
This book was set in Bembo

Printed in the United States of America

10 9 8 7 6 5 4 3 2 1

CONTENTS

FOREWORD

These are challenging times. As London shows, the world has not become a safer place since 9/11, despite president Bush's latest rationale for the Iraq War: "We're taking the fight to the terrorists abroad, so we don't have to face them here at home." Meanwhile, in the years since 9/11 we have seen our own democracy compromised by fear, hatred, and intimidation, with basic rights, due process, privacy, and the spirit of dissent undermined. It's become apparent that the occupation of Iraq, and the jingoistic and antidemocratic policies of the administration, have only made the world more dangerous.

Unfortunately, in this crucial moment the American media has not risen to the challenge of letting the truth be known. Unlike the rest of the world, we in America don't see the reality of war—the blood and gore inflicted upon our soldiers or the women and children of Iraq—because our media acquiesces in the administration's sanitizing of reality. It took an independent researcher's Freedom of Information Act request to even get photos of the coffins of dead American soldiers released by the government, and when one West Coast newspaper had the temerity to publish one of those photos, the couple who gave them the picture—they worked for a U.S. cargo contractor—were fired from their jobs.

As this book makes clear, the problem is deeper than the administration or the right-wing echo chamber on talk radio and Fox. The very structure of our conglomerated media system conspires against real journalism, and hence, against truth. And without access to truth, democracy withers.

But this book also makes clear that an extraordinary movement is growing in the country—the movement to take back the media. Thousands—hundreds of thousands—of people have determined to talk back to the media, to immerse themselves in the minutiae of FCC rules, to set up independent outlets. To let the truth be known. A couple years ago, speaking at the National Press Club, I suggested to the journalists there that they had an awesome responsibility and an awesome power: the fate of discourse and the health of the republic. In the absence of an independent media, and in this new age of the internet and new information delivering systems, that responsibility and power falls to the American people. The continuance of democracy depends on all of us.

—Tim Robbins
August 2005

TUCKER IS A WHAT?

"I'm here to confront you, because we need help from the media and they're hurting us."

—Jon Stewart, appearing on CNN's
Crossfire, 15 October 2005

The most important television interview of the 2004 campaign did not feature the grilling of a presidential contender by a skeptical and unyielding journalist. Rather, it came when Jon Stewart, the comedian who hosts Comedy Central's *The Daily Show*, appeared on *Crossfire*, the Cable News Network program that pits Democratic and Republican apologists in the daily equivalent of a partisan mud-wrestling match. Stewart was hawking a new book—which had shot to Number 1 on the bestseller lists—and he was supposed to come on *Crossfire* and crack jokes. Instead, he tore into the hosts for doing what most broadcast personalities do these days: empty the discourse of meaning and then scream and yell about the personal peccadillos of politicians, obsess about petty scandals, and generally miss the point as American democracy crumbles. Stewart was blunt about the failings of the *Crossfire* hosts ("What you do is partisan hackery"), just as he was poignant in his plea for shows such as *Crossfire* and *Hardball* to stop providing broadcast forums for the lies that representatives of the two parties tell, in places such as the "spin alleys" that are set up after presidential debates ("Now, don't you think that, for people watching at home, that's kind of a drag, that you're literally walking to a place called Deception Lane?"). *Crossfire's* conservative cohost Tucker Carlson was aghast at the criticism and, in a response that summed up the degeneration of American journalism, he attacked Stewart for not being tougher on politicians who appeared on *The Daily Show*. Stewart replied, "If your idea of confronting me is that I don't ask hard-hitting enough news questions, we're in bad shape, fellows . . . You're on CNN. The show that leads into me is puppets making crank phone calls."

Then Stewart called Carlson "a dick," which is true, and explained that "right now, you're helping the politicians and the corporations," which is even more true.

But the truest statement of all was Stewart's assertion, as a citizen rather than a comedian, that "we need help from the media, and they're hurting us."

This book is about how the media hurts America. More specifically, it is about the media crisis in the United States, a crisis in which we are seeing the deterioration of political journalism, if not its effective termination. The collapse of journalism spells disaster for any concept we might hold that this is a self-governing society, or even that citizens can fulfill the public role envisioned in our Constitution.

In this book we offer readers a framework by which to judge the role that media play in American democracy. That framework is rooted in the intentions of the founders who added a freedom of the press protection to the Bill of Rights and wrote about their intentions. We then apply that framework to today, examining media coverage of the U.S. invasion and occupation of Iraq in 2003–05 and the presidential election in 2004 (chapters 3, 4, and 5). On these two most central tests of a free press—war and the disposition of political power—our media failed miserably, with severe consequences we may not yet be able to fully imagine.

Other authors have and will provide superb critiques of media coverage of the invasion of Iraq and the 2004 presidential election. We rely upon this earlier work herein, though we also have done considerable original research, and our intent is to not only synthesize the work of others but to offer fresh insights.

But our work goes beyond a critique of media coverage in two core respects. First, the value we bring to this enterprise is that we put the current crisis in broader political context, and explain what historical factors account for our predicament (chapters 1, 2, and the first half of 3). In an immediate sense, the crisis in our journalism is due to the combination of the severe attack on professional journalism by corporate pressures to maximize profits and by the right-wing attack on the "liberal" media. But professional journalism itself is hardly a panacea. The manner in which it developed in the United States was anything but inevitable or natural. Hence, a genuine explanation of the media crisis necessitates structural and historical context.

Our institutional framework for understanding the dismal coverage of the U.S. invasion and occupation of Iraq can be applied to nearly all reporting on the American role in the world. Likewise our approach to the 2004 presidential election is applicable to other elections in the United States. Hence the subtitle of the book refers to wars and elections in the plural. This woeful media performance is due to long-term structural problems. Unless these structural problems are addressed directly, we should expect more of the same, possibly even worse, in the coverage of future invasions and elections. Without fundamental changes, this may be a book with a regrettably long shelf life.

What distinguishes this book from many critiques of media coverage is the argument that the media crisis is not due to incompetent or corrupt journalists or owners, but rather to a highly concentrated profit-driven media system that makes it rational to gut journalism and irrational to provide the content a free society so desperately requires. This media system is not natural, it does not result from a free market. Rather, it is shaped by corrupt policies and subsidies made secretly by powerful corporate interests and their political bagmen in Washington, D.C. and the state capitols. This points to the solution to the crisis: changing the media policies to create a better system, a system in which quality journalism becomes a rational expectation.

Following our logic, this is not and cannot be a book that is simply about diagnosing a fundamental political problem for the United States. Hence, the second way in which this book goes beyond being a critique of media coverage: It is about taking that diagnosis and looking for meaningful solutions. As such, it features a detailed analysis of the burgeoning popular movement to reform the media in this country, a movement fueled by indignation at the abysmal press coverage of the Iraq war and the 2004 presidential election (chapter 6). It is a movement we ourselves have participated in, and this personal experience informs our analysis. The book concludes with a concrete analysis of the three branches of the media reform movement in the United States today—criticism/education, the creation of independent media, and media policy reform—and a discussion of how they can and must complement each other. Based upon the stunning growth of media reform activism over the past three years, we analyze its strengths and weaknesses as a viable social movement.

We also reject an argument that is becoming commonplace. That argument says the Internet and other new communication technologies are blasting open the media system and slaying the dinosaur media firms of the past, so that we needn't worry about the commercial media status quo or corrupt policy making. Although we share the excitement about the potential of digital communication, in chapter 6 we explain why it is the media activism of fools to think we can use technology alone to leapfrog the crisis we are in.

While we focus upon journalism in this book, we are well aware that much political education or awareness comes from elsewhere in the media. Films, television programs, and music all inform our understanding of the world. Humor can be invaluable in helping us gain insight or keep our sanity. We are delighted, for example, to see the reception of *The Daily Show* on cable television. But we recall the words of Ralph Nader who once said the finest political satire he ever saw was in the old Soviet Union. It was so brilliant because the official media were so atrocious—yet it was hardly a desirable alternative. Viable journalism is a sine qua non for a free society.

Much of the argument we make can be extended if one wishes for the balance of the media system. The same firms that dominate journalism tend to dominate everything else, and the same corrupt policymaking that has permitted journalism to deteriorate is wreaking havoc on our media culture everywhere. For example, the commercial pressures that have leveled political journalism are part and parcel of the broader and unprecedented wave of hypercommercialism across our media and culture.

We are not making some sort of romantic argument about a proverbial lost golden age. Some of the flaws in our political journalism are deep seated and are owed to commercial control of the press and to the professional code which emerged roughly a century ago. No media system will ever be perfect. But we do believe that a rigorous accounting with history offers necessary insights and perspectives on our current situation and points the way out.

We frame the book in the terms laid down by one of America's Founding Fathers, James Madison, who, along with Thomas Jefferson, thought and wrote the most about freedom of the press. Our point is not to deify Madison or to argue that since Madison said something, it must be true. After all, Madison, like the other founders, was a man full of contradictions, with abhorrent positions on slavery, native Americans, and voting rights for women and poor white men. As much as he was obsessed with making popular governance effective and possible, he was troubled by the prospect of the lower classes controlling the polity.

But in Madison's work we find a recognition of the importance of a free press and concerns about a media system that fails to monitor military adventures that are nothing short of prescient when we apply them to our current situation. His legacy is important, too, because it reminds us that critics of the existing U.S. media system are not anti-American, or employing strange and untested foreign ideologies. On the contrary, those of us who speak for media reform do so in the language and in the best tradition of the American democratic experiment. It is the current commissars of the U.S. media system who are the interlopers; they are the ones who have betrayed democracy.

We write this book, too, with a certain amount of urgency and passion, perhaps more than that associated with our other works. This is not a time to sit idly by and claim neutrality, assert that everything is too complex to make a definitive judgment, and believe that saying something is complex therefore makes the analysis sophisticated and wondrously intellectual. When the evidence points clearly in a particular direction, when the cost of inactivity and indecision is disastrous, to be neutral is to take a stand on behalf of a corrupt and indefensible status quo.

This Americans cannot do.

Our country is in a crisis. It is time to respond to that crisis. It is time to act.

CHAPTER 1

TRAGEDY AND FARCE

"A popular Government without popular information or the means of acquiring it, is but a Prologue to a Farce or a Tragedy or perhaps both. Knowledge will forever govern ignorance, and a people who mean to be their own Governors, must arm themselves with the power knowledge gives."

—James Madison

James Madison was the most fretful founder. The crafter of the Constitution cherished the American experiment every bit as much as did the other essential men of his time, but he did not share their triumphalism. Others might be content to predict a future of easy growth and glory that would take their new nation from strength to strength, but Madison worried about the pitfalls that lay ahead. The man who served the new nation in more critical capacities than anyone save his closest comrade, Thomas Jefferson, understood the idealism of his fellows. But he also saw in the greedy and self-serving impulses of the rising political class the potential undoing of the revolutionary promise of the republic. As the coconvener (with Alexander Hamilton) of the Constitutional Convention of 1787, Madison sought to establish structures of government and to balance their powers in a way that might protect the country from the misdeeds and manipulations of men and their factions. Even after the Constitution was adopted, Madison continued to sweat the details of nation building. He became the Cassandra of the new nation, warning again and again of dangers ahead. And he did so with such insight and precision that his warnings remain in effect, and eerily appropriate, to this day.

Consider the prescience of Madison's counsel regarding presidential warmaking in light of the current crisis of the nation he brought into being: "War is in fact the true nurse of executive aggrandizement. In war a physical force is to be created, and it is the executive will which is to direct it. In war the public treasures are to be unlocked, and it is the executive hand which is to dispense them. In war the honors and emoluments of office are to be multiplied; and it is the executive patronage under which they are to be enjoyed. It is in war, finally, that laurels are to be gathered, and it is the executive brow they are to encircle. The strongest passions, and the most dangerous weaknesses of the human breast; ambition, avarice, vanity, the honorable or venial love of fame, are all in conspiracy against the desire and duty of peace." Madison understood the need for constant checks and balances against the excesses of executive power. The Congress would have its duties, as would the judiciary. But, ultimately, what in Madison's day was known as "the press" and today has become "the media" would be the most critical factor, as it alone could provide the necessary information and nurture the fundamental discourse that would maintain the democratic republic that Madison more than most of the other founders so desperately desired. It was with this understanding that Madison issued his most urgent warning: "A popular Government without popular information or the means of acquiring it, is but a Prologue to a Farce or a Tragedy or perhaps both. Knowledge will forever govern ignorance, and a people who mean to be their own Governors, must arm themselves with the power knowledge gives."

MAKING THE PRESIDENT PALATABLE

In the first years of the twenty-first century, the vitality of Madison's fear regarding what would become of his country in the absence of a free and freewheeling media has been revealed in chilling detail. America has been transformed by a scheming president and his conspiratorial aides into an empire-building enterprise where it is indeed

true that "the most dangerous weaknesses of the human breast; ambition, avarice, vanity, the honorable or venial love of fame, are all in conspiracy against the desire and duty of peace." With its Patriot Act, its Orwellian Department of Homeland Security, and, above all, its wars, the Bush administration has moved Madison's nation to the militant footing that is most easily abused by the powerful who, in order to obtain and retain political power, spin self-serving strategies into storylines grounded not in fact but in a warped version of reality that affronts much of what Americans have traditionally known and valued. So laughable have been this president's arguments for his election and reelection, and so horrific have been the results of his military misadventures, that it is difficult for most of the world to imagine how such a leader could be palatable to people who are, after all, their own governors. But, of course, George W. Bush is not palatable to the American people in raw form. He has only been made palatable by the processing of his candidacies and presidency in a media that stenographically reports the administration's spin as truth, while rejecting expressions of reality as manifestations of partisanship that must be balanced with more spin. As veteran journalist Bill Moyers noted in an address to the 2005 National Conference on Media Reform that bemoaned the present patterns in major media news programs: "Objectivity is not satisfied by two opposing people offering competing opinions, leaving the viewer to split the difference." Rather, Moyers noted in the lonely voice of the boy who asserted that the emperor had no clothes, "objective journalism means describing the object being reported on, including the little fibs and fantasies as well as the Big Lie of the people in power."

Unfortunately, while Moyers echoed the view of many working journalists, he was not speaking the language of the media barons who have, with their cost cuts and consultant-driven definitions of what is and is not news, shaped broadcast, print, and digital media into something that is more likely to spread the Big Lie than to check it.

In a nation where repeated waves of media consolidation have made a handful of multinational corporations the arbiters of public discourse, a culture of bigness has contributed to the creation of a lumbering and lazy media that is ideally suited to the smooth manipulations of White House political czar Karl Rove and the thousands of other paid liars who have become more definitional than the politicians they serve. The pathologies of unchecked deceit, injected into the body politic by a conflict-shy media, have so infected the body politic that for many Americans there no longer is popular information or the means of acquiring it. Yes, of course, the truth can be pecked out along the margins of the national debate. Yes, it is true that on some public and community radio stations, in some magazines, and on some weblogs and websites a different view of the world can be discerned. These are welcome and of growing importance, but, as we discuss herein, hardly sufficient to allay our concerns.

NO MORE TOUGH QUESTIONS

The truth is this: On the front pages of the largest newspapers, on the evening news, on the cable TV gabfests and drive-time radio talk shows that have become the town hall meetings of atomized society, the American political discourse is so empty and stilted as to be meaningless. Thus it was that in March 2003 as George W. Bush prepared to launch a preemptive war that had stirred unprecedented global controversy, he was able to hold a news conference during which the elite of the Washington press corps asked him not a single probing question about the flimsy case that had been made for war, nor about its likely costs, nor about anything akin to an exit strategy. Even some reporters who were present were appalled; ABC News White House correspondent Terry Moran said the press corps looked "like zombies," while Copley News Service Washington correspondent George Condon Jr. told *American Journalism Review* that it "just became an article of faith among a lot of people: Look at this White House press corps; it's just abdicated all responsibility." Millions of Americans agreed. "I talked to people everywhere I went who said that if the media, especially the television media, had done its job, there wouldn't have been a war," says Representative Jim McDermott (D-Washington).

That single press conference telescoped the broad failure of journalism that defined the prewar period into a single hour of shame. Among those members of the media elite who maintained a capacity for embarrassment, there would come acknowledgment of the White House press corps' atrocious performance. Two of the Republic's most prominent newspapers, the *New York Times* and the *Washington Post,* would eventually, if grudgingly, admit that they had failed to ask the right questions at the right time. But these admissions represented only the tidying up of the historical record. When America's contemporary media system faced the great challenge for which Madison and others had warned that it must be prepared—questioning the executive before the onset of war—it failed. What followed, as Madison had predicted, was tragedy, on an epic scale.

Why did the media stumble so miserably in the period before the U.S. invasion of Iraq? What was it that caused reporters and editors who had to have known better to become the mouthpieces of Bush administration deceptions and neoconservative fantasies? The best answer is that too many national-level reporters and editors have ceased to act as journalists in the sense that most Americans understand the craft. In the latter years of the nineteenth century, Joseph Pulitzer suggested that the role of the honest journalist was "to protest against the real causes of the prostrate condition of the country—the corruption, the lawlessness, the usurpation and the profligacy of [the] national administration." At the beginning of the twenty-first century, however, journalism in the sense that Pulitzer imagined it is rarely practiced. Rather, Washington-based reporters for major media companies are celebrity "content providers" who have grown concerned with playing stories safe and avoiding controversy—in hopes of retaining access to the powerful sources of the official line and the good pictures that go with such access—rather than in upholding Pulitzer's principle that journalists must "never be satisfied with merely printing the news." That the passion for access happens to protect the interests of the most politically and economically powerful individuals in the country is no coincidence. The relationship works for both the White House and the big media companies, which are no longer the combatants that they were in the days when Pulitzer's *New York World* published comments from President Theodore Roosevelt followed by the disclaimer: "To the best of the *World's* knowledge and belief, each and all of these statements made by Mr. Roosevelt and quoted above are untrue, and Mr. Roosevelt must have known they were untrue when he made them."

In the major media of America today, so blunt an assessment of a president's credibility is unimaginable, not because presidents have stopped lying but because most media outlets have stopped calling them on it. This failure leads, by its very nature, to talk of conspiracy. And there are plenty of examples of collusion between the current White House and elements of the media from the embedding of journalists with ground troops in Iraq to the eerie parallels between Bush administration talking points and FOX News reports to the attempt by Sinclair Broadcasting to air a propaganda film produced with the sole intent of destroying the president's Democratic opponent to the revelations that government agencies paid so-called journalists to peddle the party line. But conspiracy theories do not begin to explain the current crisis. The reality is that the contemporary structures of broadcast media ownership and regulation, as well as recent patterns of consolidation of newspaper ownership and the pressure on all media to turn ever-increasing levels of profit, conspire far more effectively than Karl Rove and Dan Rather ever could to undermine journalism and, ultimately, to constrain the flow of facts, ideas, and debate that is the lifeblood of democracy. Media today treats Americans as consumers, not citizens. And the theory in the boardrooms is that consumers are attracted by entertainment, rather than information. Former Vermont Governor Howard Dean, fresh from the 2004 presidential campaign trail, put it best when he said, "The media is trained to get the entertainment value and screw the facts." In such an environment, Dean's "scream" speech on the night of the Iowa caucuses gets far more attention than Dean's thoughtful critique of U.S. trade policies, even though the scream put no one but a few Dean aides out of work, while the free trade agenda of the Clinton and Bush administrations has shuttered thousands of factories and displaced millions of workers and farmers in the U.S. and abroad. The serious work of covering politics and government is treated as a burden that must be tossed off as quickly as possible in order to get down to the business of celebrity gossip about who is getting Botox injections.

KEEPING IT LIGHTWEIGHT

The pressure to keep it light has led media companies to deemphasize serious reporting, especially the sort of costly and controversial investigative reporting that gets Washington elites jittery. Thus, official spin is accepted without question, and obvious untruths are treated as reasonable statements that cannot be dismissed as deceit but can only be "balanced" by the aggrieved victims of the lies and their hapless defenders. In the process, even the most important stories become parodies of themselves. Nowhere was this more evident than in the 2004 presidential election, which should have featured a broad national debate about issues of war and peace and the direction of the American economy, but instead degenerated into a spin-driven exercise in character assassination that allowed Rove to choose the issues, define the debate, and characterize the opposition in a manner that guaranteed the reelection of a president who Americans told pollsters was leading their country in the wrong direction.

A good deal of attention was paid to the media during the course of the 2004 presidential campaign, as Michael Moore's anti–George W. Bush documentary *Fahrenheit 9/11* became the number one film in the land, the mighty CBS News operation was discredited by a manufactured scandal regarding a report on the president's very real avoidance of duty during the Vietnam War, and the armies of the Right waged a political jihad against Democratic presidential contenders on talk radio and in the media's no man's land of the Internet. There was, as well, the spectacle of a growing, but still technically and structurally feeble, opposition attempting to counter the Rush Limbaughs, Sean Hannitys, and Bill O'Reillys of the day with progressive experiments in radio and Internet innovations. Through it all, Karl Rove played out his scenarios with little or no challenge by the major media outlets that were the only institutions powerful enough to uphold the standards of truth and fair practice that are essential to democracy. The state media of the old Soviet Union was rarely so thoroughly manipulated against reality as was the supposedly free press of the United States during the course of the campaign between Bush and his Democratic challenger, Massachusetts Senator John Kerry. So it should come as little surprise that the 2004 election in the United States recalled those show elections in the Soviet Union, or that despite the fact that he had been caught telling outrageous lies, despite the fact that he had led the country into unnecessary war, despite the fact that he had left the economy in a dubious state, the incumbent was reelected. And, while that reelection was by one of the narrowest margins ever for an incumbent president, it was soon referred to in the media as a mandate not just for Bush but for a vaguely-defined moral values agenda by journalists who place more faith in self-serving White House pronouncements than the election returns. Here is the farce about which Madison warned.

So it is that we find ourselves in the Madisonian moment. Lied to by our leaders, cut off from popular information, and denied the debate that is essential to the maintenance of genuine democracy, Americans have seen the prologue to tragedy or farce. It is done. And we have been left with both, in the form of a horrific war and an absurd president. This is a book about how it happened. There are villains, to be sure. And there are heroes. But, above all, there is the fact that the crises of the current moment were made possible by a media that does not function as it was intended by the founders who wrote into our Constitution a powerful and necessary freedom of the press guarantee. That guarantee, which was supposed to assure that citizens would always have a watchdog at the ready to warn of the corruptions and crimes of the powerful, becomes meaningless when it is employed merely in the pursuit of profit by media companies that feel no responsibility to preserve and advance democracy. But while this book tells a story of tragedy and farce, it also holds out the promise of redemption and renewal.

The American people know better than the occupants of high stations in government, and the owners of the media conglomerates that have become the tribunes of a self-serving and self-absorbed political class, that Madison was right: Knowledge will forever govern ignorance, and a people who mean to be their own governors, must arm themselves with the power knowledge gives. A consciousness of the crisis is afoot in the land. Alarmed by the empty discourse that made possible an unnecessary war and shocked by the realization that the safety valve of electoral politics has been broken by a media that willingly accepts manipulation, millions of Americans are embracing the call for media reform. Their cry is being heard by honest players in politics and the media, and a revolt is in the making. If we are right that this movement is to be unstoppable, then it will be in our time that Madison's message is remade from a warning to a promise. Yes, "A popular Government without popular information or the means of acquiring it, is but a Prologue to a Farce or a Tragedy or perhaps both." We know that now. But we also know that, if we arm ourselves with the power knowledge gives, we have the ability to undo tragedy and farce. This book is not the story of the ultimate defeat of democracy. Rather, it is the record of a crisis, a crisis every bit as real as the one that Madison's compatriot Tom Paine described in his revolutionary pamphlets. If we believe in the better angels of the American experiment, then we must believe that the consciousness of the crisis will, in our day as it did in the time of Madison and Paine, inspire the revolution that will begin the world anew. So read these words not in despair but in anticipation. We can reform our media. We can make it the servant of democracy. We can make a reality that is stronger than the lies of George Bush, Dick Cheney, Karl Rove, and the corporatized communications that have served them so well. The era of tragedy and farce is closing, the era of an enraged citizenry, armed with the power that knowledge gives, is dawning. And the democracy that the first American revolution promised will be made real by the second.

CHAPTER 2

THE CRISIS IN JOURNALISM

"The functionaries of every government have propensities to command at will the liberty and property of their constituents. There is no safe deposit for these but with the people themselves, nor can they be safe with them without information. Where the press is free, and every man able to read, all is safe."

—Thomas Jefferson to Charles Yancey, 1816

A returned Jefferson, surveying the American experiment at the dawn of its third century, would be horrified at the extent to which the functionaries of our current government go unquestioned as they command at will the liberty and property not merely of their constituents but of the world. Never in the history of this country has the necessity of a free press and the free flow of information been more evident. Yet, both are under heavy assault. Bill Moyers, the most Jeffersonian of our contemporary commentators, has observed, freedom and freedom of communications were birth twins in the United States. They grew up together, and neither has fared very well in the other's absence. Boom times for the one have been boom times for the other. Yet today, despite plenty of lip service on every ritual occasion to freedom of the press, powerful forces are undermining that very freedom, damning the streams of significant public interest news that irrigate and nourish the flowering of self-determination.

Moyers is right. American journalism is in crisis. To understand the full extent of this crisis, it is important to remember the contribution that journalism is supposed to make to a free society. What was it that Jefferson and Madison had in mind when they battled at the founding of the country for freedom of the press? There is a good deal of consensus among democratic theorists on this issue. Democracy-sustaining journalism has three components: It must be a rigorous watchdog of those in power and those who wish to be in power; it must present a wide range of informed views on the most pressing issues of the day; and it must be able to expose deception and permit the truth to rise to the top. Each medium need not do all of the above, but the media system as a whole must assure that the whole package is delivered to the whole population.

The contemporary U.S. media system flunks this test, even grading on a curve. The watchdog is more often a lapdog, and huge expanses of power in our society—governmental and corporate—go unexamined in our journalism. The range of debate, such that it is on the handful of issues that receive attention, extends, as media critic Jeff Cohen likes to put it, all the way from GE to GM. And our media system has become a liar's paradise, where the cost of misrepresentation has become so low that it is now open season. In this book we measure the caliber of our journalism by looking at the two central tests of a free press: how well it monitors the warmaking power of the government and permits the citizenry to intervene to prevent military adventurism; and how well it empowers citizens to effectively conduct elections for leadership of the government. The results of those test do not present a pretty picture.

A common explanation for the crisis in our journalism is that it reflects the concentration of ownership, as giant media corporations wield inordinate power over journalism. Others argue that it reflects the decline in objective reporting and the rise of partisanship, be it from the Left or Right. And many point to the centuries-old reluctance of governments—even elected governments—to operate in the sunshine of disclosure and criticism. In fact, the state of contemporary journalism is not due exclusively to any of the above factors, but to the confluence of a number of structural factors, some of which date back more than a century, even to the nation's founding. They came to a head in recent years in the form of rabid commercial pressures on

the autonomy and integrity of professional journalism, combined with a well-organized and -funded right-wing attack on the "liberal" media. In this chapter we trace this process.

RISE OF PROFESSIONAL JOURNALISM

It comes as a surprise to many to learn that the notion of objectivity or simply professional journalism is a relatively recent development in the United States. In the first one hundred-plus years of the republic, journalism tended to be highly opinionated and partisan. Indeed, the first few generations of U.S. journalists—the years from Madison and Jefferson to Jackson and Lincoln—were diametrically opposed to what many Americans think is intended by the First Amendment: a commitment to neutral, values-free news reporting. Horace Greeley did not write, "Both the East and the West have their relative merits for a recent college grad"; he wrote, "Go West, young man." And that was not his only pronouncement. Greeley's *New York Tribune,* the great American journal of the mid-nineteenth century, was never neutral. It prodded the still-new nation to address the sin of slavery, to consider the dangers of imperialism and to recognize the need to provide for the common welfare. Greeley's writers were anything but impartial observers; one of his regular correspondents, and arguably among the greatest journalists of the nineteenth century, was a German scholar named Karl Marx. The *Tribune* was typical of its times and, with other newspapers of its kind, essential to the progress that America achieved in the period of transition from revolutionary republic to global superpower.

In recent journalism history textbooks, this period, especially the decades immediately following independence, has been referred to as the Dark Ages of American journalism—with the premise that the less said about it, the better. Upon closer inspection, however, it becomes clear that partisan journalism had its strengths, not the least of which was its tendency to contextualize political issues so that citizens could recognize seemingly random events as part of a coherent pattern. Such an approach tends to draw people into public life. Observers note that nations around the world with partisan press systems tend to have high voter turnouts and more passionate political cultures. In the United States, the high-water mark for partisan journalism was arguably the 1820s and 1830s, and in the northern states this era is characterized as one of broad democratic participation among those who were allowed to vote.

Partisan press systems have their clear downside, too. After all, the press systems of Nazi Germany and the Soviet Union were partisan. A partisan press can degenerate into shameless lying and blatant propaganda, the purpose of which is to depoliticize the citizens rather than engage them. The key to having partisan journalism promote democratic values, rather than repress them, is to have a wide range of partisan viewpoints available, and for it to be feasible to launch a new partisan newspaper or magazine if one is dissatisfied with the existing range of options. One way to view the freedom of the press clause in the First Amendment is to see that it protects the right of citizens to launch their own publications, even if they are opposed to the political views of those holding political power at the time. That radical idea was mainstream thinking at the time of the country's founding.

Until the middle of the nineteenth century, massive postal and printing subsidies assured that there was a range of newspapers and magazines in circulation far beyond what market forces would have permitted. Over the course of the nineteenth century, as publishing became an increasingly lucrative sector, market competition generated innumerable new newspapers, with publishers seeking profit as much or more than political influence. This was a classic competitive market, where new entrepreneurs could enter the field and launch a newspaper with relative ease if they were dissatisfied with the existing publications. Major cities like New York or Chicago or St. Louis tended to have well over a dozen daily newspapers at any given time, reflecting a fairly broad range of political viewpoints. The system was far from perfect, yet it worked.

But built within the commercial press system of the late nineteenth century were the seeds of its own destruction, which led to the greatest crisis in U.S. journalism until the one we are in the midst of today. On the one hand, as newspapering became an explicitly commercial enterprise, political journalism was no longer privileged per se, as the point was to generate as many readers as possible as inexpensively as possible. This led to the rise of sensationalism, blatant fabrication of stories, widespread bribing of journalists, and all sorts of other disreputable measures that undermined the legitimacy of journalism.

On the other hand, as newspapering became big business, markets became much less competitive. By the early twentieth century, there were fewer and fewer newspapers in any given community, and in many towns there remained only one or two competing dailies. Barriers to entry emerged that made it virtually impossible to launch a new newspaper in a community, even if the existing papers were highly profitable. In short, newspaper publishing became monopolistic, far more so than most other major industries. Indeed, there has not been a single profitable new daily newspaper established in the United States in an existing market since World War I, despite the growth of the nation and the exceptional profitability in the industry overall.

This led to a political crisis for journalism. It was one thing for newspapers to be stridently partisan when there were numerous competing voices and when it was not impossible to launch a new newspaper if the existing range was unsatisfactory. It was altogether different when there were only one or two newspapers and it was impossible to start a new one. Moreover, as the papers were larger and the owners were always wealthy, the politics tended to be antilabor and probusiness. In community after community, newspapers were in bed with those who owned and controlled the community. In this context partisanship reeked of the heavy-handedness one associates with authoritarian regimes, or, to be more accurate, company towns.

During the first decades of the twentieth century, the crisis spawned by sensationalism and right-wing crony partisanship reached a boiling point. In the 1912 presidential race, all three challengers to President William Howard Taft—Democrat Woodrow Wilson, Progressive Theodore Roosevelt, and Socialist Eugene Debs—criticized the corruption and venality of the press. It was in this cauldron of controversy that professional journalism was spawned. A driving force was the publishers themselves who understood that partisan and sensationalistic journalism was undermining their business model. They had to accept self-regulation to protect their profits and to ward off the threat of organized public-reform efforts.

Professional journalism was the solution to the crisis. It was the revolutionary idea that the owner and editor of a newspaper would be split, and a "Chinese Wall" put between them. News would no longer be shaped to suit the partisan interests of press owners, but rather would be determined by trained nonpartisan professionals, using judgment and skills honed in journalism schools. There were no such schools in 1900; by the end of World War I nearly every major journalism school in the nation had been established, often at the behest of newspaper owners. Professionalism meant that the news would appear the same whether the paper was owned by a Republican or a Democrat. Professionalism meant that there was no longer any reason to be concerned about the monopolistic nature of newspaper markets since owners would not abuse their power and, besides, so the theory went, more newspapers in the same community would merely reproduce the same professional content, so they were redundant.

PROFESSIONAL JOURNALISM: PROS AND CONS

The strengths of professionalism are self-evident. It gives editors and reporters a measure of independence from the owners' politics and from commercial pressures to shape the news to please advertisers and the bottom line. It places a premium on being fair and upon being accurate. It makes it a cardinal sin, a career killer, to accept bribes or to fabricate stories. No wonder so many Americans think that the problem with U.S. journalism is that there is too little objectivity, as professional journalism is often characterized albeit inaccurately. (Even the strongest proponents of neutral journalism now recognize that values play a crucial role in story selection, deciding what gets covered and what does not, not to mention how the coverage is framed. Journalists covering a story can never be objective in the sense of a number of mathematicians who would all come up with the same answer for a problem. Instead of objectivity, the preferred terms today are fairness, accuracy, and balance.)

Professionalism looked awfully good compared to what it replaced and was largely welcomed across the board. Yet criticism of the weaknesses of professional journalism and its biases began almost immediately, and by the second half of the twentieth century had become widespread in both journalists' memoirs and in sociological criticism of the news. As Ben Bagdikian famously put it, the core problems with professional journalism as it developed in the United States are threefold: 1) reliance on official sources; 2) fear of context; 3) a dig here, not there, built-in bias concerning what areas of power are fair game and what are off-limits.

Professional journalism places a premium on legitimate news stories based upon what people in power say and do. The appeal is clear. It removes the tinge of controversy from story selection—"Hey, the Governor said it so we had to cover it"—and it makes journalism less expensive: Simply place reporters near people in power and have them report on what is said and done. It also gives journalism a very conventional feel, as those in power have a great deal of control over what gets covered and what does not. Reporting often turns into dictation as journalists are loathe to antagonize their sources, depending upon them as they do for stories. Indeed, successful politicians learn to exploit journalists' dependence upon official sources to maximum effect. This dependence also makes possible what the modern public-relations industry does in its surreptitious manner.

The best-case scenario for journalists relying on official sources is when people in power have strong debates over fundamental issues, providing a good deal of wiggle room in which journalists can operate. The 2005 debate over privatizing Social Security is a good example, as President Bush and leading Democrats squared off in opposite corners. The worst-case scenario, where those in power are in general agreement and are not debating an issue, is a nightmare for democratic journalism. If journalists raise an issue that no one in power is debating, they are instantly accused of being ideological and unprofessional and attempting to force their own views into the news. It is criticism few journalists enjoy—it can be a career killer—so the reliance on official sources has a tremendous disciplinary effect on the range of legitimate news stories. It also means the public is at the mercy of those in power to a far greater extent than was the case under partisan journalism.

Context is often eschewed by professional journalism because it opens the door to the charge of partisanship. It is awfully difficult to contextualize a story well without showing some partisan inclinations or making some controversial value judgments. So professional journalism tends to pummel people with facts, but rarely pummels people with a nuanced appreciation of what the facts might mean. This helps explain the numerous studies that show that sustained consumption of the news on a particular subject often does not lead to a better understanding of the subject and sometimes leads to more confusion. Which means that professional news can have the ironic effect of making public life more confusing and less interesting and attractive, thereby promoting depoliticization. This is one area where professional journalism as it developed in the United States stands in direct contrast to its partisan predecessor. If nothing else, partisan journalism put stories in context and attempted to find the common thread between them.

"Dig here, not there" refers to the implicit or unspoken biases built into the professional code. They tend to be the biases that are favored by media owners, and journalists who climb the organizational ladder tend to be those who have the least problem internalizing them. For example, it is unusual for local news media to do hard-hitting critical examinations of the most powerful families and commercial institutions in their own communities. It is one of the great weak spots of our journalism, because if the local media in Decatur, Illinois, do not investigate the big shots of Decatur, it is highly unlikely the local news media of Fresno, California, will send a delegation of reporters to Decatur to do the job for them.

At a more macro level, as Bagdikian points out, our news media have internalized the notion that corporate power is largely benevolent, capitalism is synonymous with democracy, and the United States is a force for good in the world. So it is that corporate malfeasance gets barely a sniff of investigative journalism, unless blatant transgressions affect investors, while stories concerning governmental malfeasance, especially in programs intended to benefit the poor and working class, are stock-in-trade.

When professional journalism is looked at in this light, it can be seen as a mixed blessing. Not only does professional journalism have biases, it has the audacity to insist that it is unbiased. This has driven critics almost to the point of insanity over the years. It is also important to note that the problems we chronicle with election and war coverage in chapters 3, 4, and 5 are due, in significant part, to problems with the professional code; they are not due strictly to the attacks on professionalism that we turn to below.

Some have concluded, after a rigorous accounting of the flaws in professional journalism, that we would be far better to return to a more explicitly partisan form of journalism. Let's cut the flawed pretense of neutrality and professionalism, the reasoning goes, and let all sides have at it. The problem with this argument is that it accepts the premise that the type of professional journalism that emerged in the United States is the only type possible, and the only alternative to it is explicit partisanship. In fact, there was a major debate in the 1930s over what constituted professional journalism between the newly formed journalists' union, the Newspaper Guild, and the press barons. To George Seldes and Heywood Broun of the Newspaper Guild, the reliance upon official sources and the internalization of the owners' biases was anathema to genuine professional journalism. They argued that a truly independent journalism required journalists to stand outside of partisan institutions assuming the perspective of those outside of power. As the legendary expression goes, journalism should "afflict the comfortable and comfort the afflicted."

For Seldes's vision of independent professional journalism to take hold, it would require that journalists use their union to prevent owners from having any control over the editorial contents of the paper, to make the Chinese Wall impermeable, and for the staff to be accountable directly to the public. Unfortunately, Seldes and the Newspaper Guild lost this fight to the extent it was ever much in play. By the 1940s the Guild became a conventional trade union, and what we know as professional journalism was on the verge of being adopted by all U.S. news media with the exception of a few cranky holdouts, like William Loeb in New Hampshire. But the Seldes vision of independent professional journalism has survived on the margins, in the work of journalists such as Seymour Hersh, Bill Moyers, Charles Lewis, and Amy Goodman, to mention but a few. It is dismissed as partisan by those who dislike the glaring light of public attention upon those in power, and because sympathy with those out of power is regarded as unacceptably ideological. But what makes this journalism so powerful is that it actually applies the same hard look at all in power regardless of party affiliation.

Professional journalism enjoyed a golden age of sorts in the late 1960s and 1970s. Although there was sharp criticism of mainstream journalism during this period in the alternative press, and in journalism reviews edited by working reporters, the resources, autonomy, and institutional strength of professional journalism were arguably at their peak during these years. On the heels of the Watergate scandal and the Nixon resignation, professional journalism enjoyed considerable prestige and was regarded as a central force for good in the nation. In the classic 1970s film drama *Three Days of the Condor,* the film ends with Robert Redford's character entering the *New York Times* building to turn over his evidence of government chicanery. The insinuation was that journalists would slay the dragon and we would all live happily ever after.

A more contemporary Hollywood drama on journalism, *The Insider,* a few years ago told the true story of how management pressure led CBS News to spike an interview with a tobacco industry whistleblower. Today, the expectation that journalists could or would provide a happy ending turns out to be unrealistic, unless the film is a farce.

THE COMMERCIAL ASSAULT ON JOURNALISM

Since the 1970s, professional journalism has been under sharp attack on two fronts. First, a wave of media consolidation and conglomeration combined with loosened federal regulations unleashed a commercial attack on the autonomy of professional journalism. Increasingly, the deal between media owners and journalists—the Chinese Wall separating church and state, commercial interests from journalistic values—no longer made as much business sense to the owners. Why should they lavish resources on news divisions unless those divisions generated the same returns as the other branches of the corporate empire? After all, the argument went, this is a business, not a charity, which must be accountable to shareholders' needs for profit maximization above all else. If the market does not encourage journalism, then people must not want or need journalism, or at least the quaint old journalism of yesteryear. Because the deal between owners and journalists was never in writing, it has eroded under steady commercial pressure.

Understood in this context, much of what has transpired in journalism over the past two or three decades makes sense. On the one hand, there has been a decrease in resources for journalism. On the other hand, journalism standards for what is considered a legitimate story have gradually transformed to incorporate the newly commercialized environment. All in all, the autonomy of professional journalism is disappearing in a manner similar to the Amazon rainforest or the ozone layer.

The reduction in resources for journalism has been widely chronicled. It means many fewer resources for investigative reporting. Roberta Baskin, who has won seventy-five awards and two Peabodys with ABC and CBS, among others, says that investigative journalism became the first area cut over the past two decades as corporate values conquered the newsroom. Moreover, investigative journalism went from being a protected and encouraged entity, to something viewed by corporate managers with suspicion. "The lawyers for the media firms have always checked our stories for possible legal issues," Baskin states. "But whereas the lawyers were once sympathetic, playing an advocacy role to the journalists and trying to get their stories on the air, now they're representing the perspective of the owners, that investigative journalism is a lot of trouble and the less of it the better." As Charles Lewis has noted, much of what passes for investigative journalism today simply involves an insider leaking a story to a reporter.

International coverage is also on the kill list. Expensive correspondents produce lots of red ink and very little black ink. Veteran

CBS News foreign correspondent Tom Fenton wrote a devastating account of the decline of international coverage in the U.S. media, especially television news, in his 2005 book, *Bad News*. Fenton notes that the amount of coverage in U.S. newspapers and on TV news devoted to foreign affairs dropped by 70 to 80 percent in the 1980s and 1990s. Fenton outlines in depressing detail the utter lack of interest corporate media executives have in covering the world. By the time the 9/11 attacks occurred, the news media had left the American public with no grounding to evaluate what had taken place and why. An American arguably had to devote enormous attention to scouring obscure sites on the Internet or pursue an advanced degree in international politics in order to have the same sense of the world that many Europeans had from exposure to their mainstream media. And despite a lot of hot air immediately following the 9/11 attacks that the news media would begin to cover the world again, such rhetoric was never taken seriously by corporate media managers.

The reduction in the number of reporters overall means increased reliance upon public relations news releases as the basis for news stories. On television, journalism is replaced by uninformed punditry and pointless prognostication, an inexpensive and entertaining way to maximize profit, but nothing remotely close to journalism. Indeed, the real revolution brought on by the FOX News Channel is less its turn to partisanship as it is its replacement of costly journalism with relatively inexpensive pundit blowhards. It is a winning business model, and highly attractive to all media owners. The other alternative is the outright elimination of news, as has happened on many radio stations and on a growing number of television stations. In town after town, there are barely a handful of journalists on the job, and issues of considerable importance get only cursory mention or no treatment whatsoever.

This means that the traditional malady of professional journalism, that it basically reports debates between elites, becomes a cancer. It is one thing to report on debates and then do some investigation, some journalism, to ascertain what the truth of the matter is. It is quite another thing to report on debates and competing claims and wash one's hands of any responsibility to examine the claims. In journalism today it is increasingly the rule that if a journalist challenges a politician's claim, they are accused of being partisan, which is anathema. It is left to the politician's opponent to make the challenge and produce the evidence, not the journalist. But since a political opponent can always be dismissed as partisan, a politician can lie with impunity. Journalists spend much more time evaluating whether politicians can successfully spin the public—i.e., lie—than they do holding politicians responsible for lying. Our journalistic environment today is a liar's paradise.

"The conventional rules of beltway journalism," as Bill Moyers put it in May 2005, "divide the world into Democrats and Republicans, liberals and conservatives, and allow journalists to pretend they have done their job if, instead of reporting the truth behind the news, they merely give each side an opportunity to spin the news. . . . Instead of acting as filters for readers and viewers, sifting the truth from the propaganda, reporters and anchors attentively transcribe both sides of the spin invariably failing to provide context, background, or any sense of which claims hold up and which are misleading."

The other side of the coin is that the standards for what is a legitimate news story have softened. Make no mistake: The trend to cover celebrities and crime, to promote advertisers, is rooted in the earliest purely commercial ventures in publishing and was in full view before the middle of the nineteenth century. As journalism became an increasingly explicit commercial enterprise, political coverage faded to be replaced by less expensive, politically trivial, and salacious fare. One of the core contributions of professional journalism was to put this commercial impulse in its place, to say that public service values needed to drive story selection and development as much as explicitly commercial values, and that these decisions needed to be the province of journalists.

At its most corrupt, journalism has increasingly been used to promote a parent company's ventures, or to promote an advertiser.

But the more striking change has been the slow internalization of the view that stories about celebrities, about lurid crime and sex, about fluff, legitimately constitute a significant amount of what can be in the diet of a respectable news outlet. This has been a recurring theme in the many memoirs published by prominent journalists over the past decade. Bonnie M. Anderson, for two decades a journalist at NBC News and CNN, wrote an extraordinary account about the collapse of journalistic values and the rise of corporate-driven info-tainment in her 2004 book, *News Flash*. She concluded that the push for profit is destroying journalism.

So it is that in 2005, as major crises loomed at home and abroad, many more Americans were immersed in news coverage of Michael Jackson's trial, Martha Stewart's probation terms, and Natalee Hollo-way's disappearance than they were in coverage of U.S. torture, or in the corruption of politics in their communities or in Washington, D.C. Not only are celebrity and fluff stories relatively inexpensive and easy to cover, not only do they easily generate an audience, they are also politically insignificant, so they ruffle no powerful feathers, ex-cept those of wayward celebrities. They give the illusion of contro-versy, but over politically insignificant events. And the more people are exposed to this coverage, the more they develop a taste for it. We confess that after being immersed in O. J. Simpson trial coverage 24/7 in 1995, even we were interested in knowing whether or not profes-sional houseguest Kato Kaelin would ever get a job.

But the motor force for this process is supply driven, not demand driven. It is simply a lot cheaper to cover celebrity misdeeds than to produce quality investigative journalism or international coverage, so it has to clear a lower bar to get embraced by the money guys running the news divisions. Baskin recounts her experience at ABC where executives would study the ratings for the news-magazine programs on a minute-by-minute basis, to see what stories, what language, what anchor, generated the best audience that could be sold to adver-tisers. Commercial values drove the journalism unabashedly. Finally, ABC decided that viewers were no longer interested in national politics, so it closed its Washington offices for *20/20,* its flagship prime-time news magazine show. "From now on," ABC informed its reporters, "we focus on personalities, pop culture, and 'big gets.'" Big gets is the corporate journalism term for a mother lode sensationalist story combining personalities, scandal and pop culture—like getting an interview with Michael Jackson or a home video of Winona Ryder shoplifting.

All of this comes to a head in local television news, which due to commercial pressures barely produces anything remotely associated with journalism as proffered at the outset of this chapter. Surveys continue to show local TV news is a leading source of information for a high percentage of Americans. Only a few minutes spent viewing any of these newscasts makes Americans' reliance upon them a sobering thought. For example, coverage of local political campaigns has all but fallen off the map at local TV newscasts. In 2004, according to a study by the Norman Lear Center, less than 10 percent of local newscasts mentioned local races in the month leading up to Election Day, and in those stories only one-third of them mentioned actual issues in the race. The United States is a very diverse nation; in Queens, New York, alone there are scores of different languages spoken and every religion and political ideology under the sun. Yet the one thing that unites all Americans in our diverse age is that every American seems to think their local TV news is the worst in the nation. No one can believe it could be worse anywhere else.

The commercial pressure on journalism also reinforces the class bias of the news. Under professionalism, journalism is regarded as a public service of value to the entire population. In theory, stories of importance to a vast number of poor or working class people should be at least as valued as stories of interest to a much smaller number of upper-middle class or rich people. This principle struggled even during the golden age of professional journalism and has been entirely abandoned over the past two decades. News is pitched primarily to the middle and upper class, the people advertisers are most interested in reaching. Labor news has disappeared. Political journalism about poor people only rates a sniff if what happens to them affects rich people. Business and investment news, pitched at maybe the top 10 or 20 percent of the nation's income earners, has exploded because it is so profitable. (As for the quality of business journalism, the less said the better: It missed the massive corporate scandals of the late 1990s because it was too busy saluting the heroes of the new economy . . . like Enron and WorldCom.)

The vantage point of U.S. journalism is from the top of the social pecking order and looking down. Our news has been turned on its head and today proudly comforts the comfortable. As with the King in *The 500 Hats of Bartholomew Cubbins,* once you look much past the top of the hill, the picture gets awfully fuzzy, and the people get awfully small.

The commercial attack on professional journalism has made journalism increasingly irrelevant to Americans' lives, and people, especially young people, increasingly tune it out. It increases the ironic effect that traditional professional journalism has of discouraging public participation in civic life, rather than encouraging it. David Mindich chronicles this process in his superb book, *Tuned Out: Why Americans Under 40 Don't Follow the News.* Tragically, as Davis Merritt and Gene Roberts, among others, have chronicled, the response of media owners to declining readerships and audiences is not to devote increased resources to hard-hitting and provocative journalism, but, rather, to accept the depoliticization journalism has encouraged as irreversible and to devote ever more resources to entertainment, celebrity, and lifestyle journalism. In doing so, the commercial news media both confirm and guarantee their own unimportance.

Perhaps the most striking measure of the decline of professional journalism comes from working journalists themselves. At the height of the golden age in the 1970s, journalists often were regarded as arrogant, so great was their self-satisfaction, and so convinced were they of the important role they played in our society. Their memoirs were those of democratic warriors, on a mission from God, or at least from the Founding Fathers. By the 1990s a sea change had occurred and journalists were marinated in disillusionment with the commercial destruction of their calling. This change has been documented at some length and in considerable detail. In 2005, Laurie Garrett, one of the nation's most respected reporters, quit her job at the widely respected newspaper, *Newsday*. "All across America news organizations have been devoured by massive corporations—and allegiance to stockholders, the drive for higher share prices, and push for larger dividend returns trumps everything that the grunts in the newsrooms consider their missions," Garrett wrote in her letter of resignation, where she announced she was leaving the field. "This is terrible for democracy. I have been in forty-seven states of the U.S.A. since 9/11 and I can attest to the horrible impact the deterioration of journalism has had on the national psyche. I have found America a place of great and confused fearfulness."

Garrett is not alone. Unions and associations that represent working journalists are now among the most ardent critics of the current media system, and as we travel the country to talk about media issues we are constantly stopped by journalists who tell us, "It's even worse than you think." Working journalists are in despair at the degeneration of their craft, and Garrett is not the only one who has responded to that despair by punching out. When they do, they are giving up more than mere jobs. The poignant words that Garrett employed to explain her decision reminds us of something that should never be forgotten. Most of the people who enter journalism do so for the best of reasons. Many of them remain dedicated to doing the best possible work. The degree of difficulty they face is simply much higher than it was a few decades ago, and it is increasing before our eyes. In fact, a surprising amount of very good work still gets done, but it has less impact and tends to create very little of an echo effect. Serious journalism is on the defensive. There is far too little institutional support or encouragement for the journalism our society so desperately requires. We also should not lose sight of the fact that these institutional changes were not the natural workings of the free market. They were as much the result of corrupt and secretive policy changes—like eliminating the cap on the number of radio stations a single company could own nationally—that gave firms more leverage to jettison journalism.

RIGHT-WING CRITIQUE OF "LIBERAL" MEDIA

The other blade in the scissors that has gelded professional journalism is the right-wing attack on the "liberal" news media. The conservative critique of "liberal" news media would have been nonsensical in the preprofessional era. Then the news explicitly reflected the viewpoints of the owners, and while some were liberal and one or two radical, most were decidedly conservative. It was the emergence of professional journalism and the granting of limited autonomy to the newsroom from the owner that is the foundation of the right-wing critique. At a rhetorical level, the right-wing media critique has claimed that its goal is to make journalism more balanced and objective; its more calculating and Machiavellian advocates, like Newt Gingrich, acknowledge that the whole point has always been to make the newsroom more passive and more aligned with the political agenda of the media owners. To the extent journalism veered away from the politics of the owners, it veered to the left, and that, the Gingrichites argued, was bad.

The conservative critique of the liberal media emerged dramatically in the 1970s, when the right was convinced that news coverage was too sympathetic to liberals, blacks, environmentalists, feminists, unions, and peace activists, and insufficiently supportive of big business, religious conservatives, the military, and Republicans. The impetus for the critique was neoliberal: The conservatives wanted more charitable press coverage of conservative attempts to dismantle the welfare state, reduce health and safety regulation, lower taxes on corporations and the wealthy, and weaken the effectiveness of organized labor. Ever since, considerable resources have been devoted to pushing the news media to the right. Right-wing media "watchdogs" are

now constantly criticizing the media for being liberal, with the aim of "working the refs" like a basketball coach, as a Republican leader once put it, so that browbeaten journalists will be easier on the Right and harder on the Left. Almost anytime a major news story suggests conservatives or corporations are flawed, one can expect a chorus of howls about liberal bias. This incessant criticism has contributed to making the idea that the news media are liberal common in mainstream culture.

This conservative campaign involved much more than aggressive jawboning. It also included establishing think tanks like the American

Enterprise Institute and the Heritage Foundation to provide journalists with "experts" always touting the correct political line. It included funding numerous conservative papers on college campuses to breed a crop of right-wing journalists. It included developing a coordinated informal network of right-wing commercial media, ranging from talk radio and Sinclair Broadcasting to the *Wall Street Journal* editorial page, the *Washington Times,* and the FOX News Channel—all operating in ideological lockstep. Such partisanship is defended, with no sense of irony, on the grounds that conservative broadcasts and publications must be biased to balance mainstream journalism's failure to be unbiased.

While the scope of the right-wing campaign to manipulate journalism has been impressive, the actual intellectual argument that is offered to support it is chock full of holes and inconsistencies. The basic argument has three core elements: 1) journalists have complete control over the news; 2) journalists are liberals; and 3) journalists use their control over the news to push their liberal agenda.

The first point is preposterous and fails to survive any analysis of how news is produced, which is why even conservatives in academia rarely embrace this argument. Commercial pressures and the influence of ownership prerogatives go a long way toward shaping what is news. Newsrooms are not hippie communes where decisions get made beneath a waft of bong smoke. Owners control the budgets and set the priorities, and the top people they hire internalize the owners' values if they wish to have successful careers. It is Organizational Sociology 101. In some respects the situation is not unlike the newsroom in *Pravda* or *Tass* in the old Soviet Union. There was rarely explicit state or Communist Party repression of journalists in those newsrooms—journalists often did what they did without overt pressure—but no one claimed journalists actually had ultimate control over the Soviet media.

Conservatives understand that media owners call the shots, as was shown in the 1980s, when a right-wing group tried to purchase CBS with an announced goal to "become Dan Rather's boss." In recent years, during which the professional autonomy of journalism has been strangled by commercial pressures, the notion that journalists have more power over the news than owners is absurd.

The second point has the most empirical support; surveys consistently show that journalists tend to be more liberal than the public at large in their beliefs on social issues like abortion and gay rights. But surveys also show that the Washington press corps is more conservative than the public on economic issues: trade, corporate power, healthcare, Social Security, etc. And the further up the pecking order one goes, the more likely journalists are to adopt the politics of their class. Indeed, the great demographic change among journalists in the past fifty years has been how comfortable the top echelon of editors and reporters is moving in the corridors of power. This hardly suggests that the commercial news media are spawning angry dissidents. Those types get weeded out fairly early on.

The third point greatly overstates whatever saliency the personal liberal views of journalists might have on the news. It is an obsession of professionalism for journalists to keep their personal agendas from the news. This is why professional journalism is held hostage by official sources. If professional journalism has a clear ideological bias, it is toward those in power, the safest ground to occupy. It means that mainstream journalists are flat-footed and playing defense, obsessed with not appearing unfair to conservatives, and having far fewer qualms about sticking it to wimpy liberals. Meanwhile, the right-wing media have no qualms about being aggressively partisan for their team.

By the end of the 1990s, the long conservative campaign against real reporting had combined with the commercial pressures on professional autonomy to produce a journalism that was basically putty in the Right's hands. As the Republicans gained greater political power, and as the Democrats became considerably more probusiness under Clinton, the official sources that play such a large role in shaping what news is moved rightward too. The right-wing media often became the agenda setters for what would be talked about and what would be ignored. Consider the amount and nature of coverage of factually paired examples—e.g., Bush's military/draft record vs. Kerry's or Clinton's record, Bush's financial history vs. Clinton's, Bush's failures on 9/11 and in tracking down bin Laden vs. Jimmy Carter's handling of the Iran hostage crisis, to mention a few. The differences in coverage are striking. The Right now controls the news cycle in the United States, and there is little independent journalism challenging it. This is a theme to which we will return in the coming chapters.

It is important to note that the attack on professional journalistic autonomy from the commercial side and from the political side complement each other. The same political figures that bellyache about the "liberal" media are in bed with the corporations that own them and carry their water for them in Washington, D.C. Leading media owners like Rupert Murdoch and John Malone bankroll right-wing think tanks that bash the "liberal" media. In some respects the right-wing attack is less on liberalism, than it is on investigative journalism that reveals what Republicans in power are actually doing. And all journalism critical of Republicans in power, regardless of the evidence marshaled, is invariably dismissed as reflecting liberal bias and therefore illegitimate. As professional values erode under commercial pressure, as journalism diminishes, the door is opened to increasing the partisanship of the news, and the Right is poised to see that any increase in partisanship favors its agenda.

It is difficult not to regard the conservative campaign against the "liberal" media as anything but a brazenly opportunistic and unprincipled exercise in propaganda. On the one hand, never to our knowledge have conservative critics chastised the media for being unfair to those not on the political right. Never do conservative critics say "Hey, go easy on Kerry or Clinton or Dean, because you should hold them to the same milquetoast standard we insist upon for Bush." Whatever advances the conservative agenda is good journalism to Rush Limbaugh and FOX News; whatever undermines it is bad journalism. On the other hand, even as the Right basically has become the assignment editor for the news media, conservatives persist with the preposterous claim that the news is dominated by a bunch of wacky leftists. The myth of the liberal media must be perpetuated as a fig leaf to provide cover and justification for the stridently partisan attack in which they are engaged.

PUTTING JOURNALISM IN CONTEXT

We concede that this has been a sweeping discussion of journalism, and we have had to use broad brush strokes. We believe our core argument survives more detailed examination, and it would certainly be qualified and enriched by more detail and nuance. Likewise, we believe that the complexity of factors that explain the crisis in journalism is matched at the other end by the complexity in finding solutions to the problem. There are solutions, but there is no single button we can push to make everything right in the world of journalism or media. That is the topic of chapter 6.

We must also emphasize that, as important as the media are, they are not the sole factor in the decline of democracy in the United States today. With regard to the sorry state of our electoral system, dreadful and increasingly non-existent coverage of issues and races simply combines with corrupt campaign financing, antidemocratic election laws, and gerrymandering to effectively reduce popular involvement to the bare minimum. In the case of the U.S. role in the world, the media play a more central role, as they are the main conduit to the world for most Americans. But there is little within the media structure—aside from the fact that defense contractors own some of it and the military-industrial complex provides advertising revenues and markets to much of it—that requires the United States to have such a massive military presence worldwide. This is due to other, equally deep, structural factors.

This is an important point for the media analysis we present in the next three chapters. The Madisonian test of journalism, of a free press, is not whether it generates a democracy and prevents unnecessary wars. That is too much of a burden to place on any institution, even one as central as the media. The test of a society's journalism and media is how they address the existing balance of forces within society. Does the press, on balance, tend to challenge or reinforce antidemocratic tendencies within the broader political economy and culture? Does the press system empower people or demobilize them? Does the press allow a president to manipulate his country into an unnecessary war? Does the press system reduce the most important presidential election of a generation to a petty squabble over old military records?

We begin to answer those questions by turning again to Bill Moyers, who has said of our age, "Never has there been an administration so disciplined in secrecy, so precisely in lockstep in keeping information from the people at large and—in defiance of the Constitution— from their representatives in Congress. Never has so powerful a media oligopoly—the word is Barry Diller's, not mine—been so unabashed in reaching like Caesar for still more wealth and power. Never have hand and glove fitted together so comfortably to manipulate free political debate, sow contempt for the idea of government itself, and trivialize the people's need to know. When the journalist-historian Richard Reeves was once asked by a college student to define 'real news,' he answered: 'The news you and I need to keep our freedoms.' When journalism throws in with power, that's the first news marched by censors to the guillotine. The greatest moments in the history of the press came not when journalists made common cause with the state but when they stood fearlessly independent of it."

By any measure, this is not one of the great moments in the history of the press. It is, in fact, the antithesis of the ideals of Jefferson and Madison.

CHAPTER 3

OH, WHAT AN EMBEDDED WAR

"No nation could preserve its freedom in the midst of continual warfare."

—James Madison, 1793

Michael Powell, who then served as George W. Bush's chairman of the Federal Communications Commission (FCC), provided his assessment of media coverage of the U.S. invasion and occupation of Iraq in March 2003. It was, Powell said, "thrilling to see the power of the media." There is no question that the war provides a fine illustration of "the power of the media." But "thrilling" is not the word to describe it. "Haunting" works, although the most appropriate word is probably "terrifying."

Two fundamental political tests can be used to evaluate the caliber of a media system and the journalism it spawns. The first test measures how the press system covers elections, providing the information citizens need to determine who will hold political power and who will not. The second test involves how the press system enables citizens to monitor the government's war-making powers. War is the most serious use of state power: organized, sanctioned violence. How well it is under citizen review and control is not only a litmus test for the media but for society as a whole.

As we discussed in chapter 1, it would be difficult to exaggerate how deeply concerned our founders were with limiting the war-making power of the government, and with keeping the president in particular under strict control by Congress. The founders, most notably Madison, understood that history from Greece and Rome to modern times had repeatedly demonstrated that no society could survive for long as both a militaristic empire, defined by secrecy and hierarchy, and a self-governing republic. And they understood that a viable free press was the only mechanism that could provide citizens with the precious commodity most frequently denied them by their governors: the information necessary to control those with the power to send the nation's children to their deaths on distant killing fields.

There have been many superb and detailed analyses of U.S. media coverage of the role the United States plays in world affairs, like recent works by Nancy Snow, Robert Entman, Jon Western, and Jonathan Mermin. Already there have been compelling book-length treatments of the media's role in the country's buildup to the invasion and occupation of Iraq—like those of Danny Schechter, Sheldon Rampton and John Stauber, Norman Solomon, and Paul Rutherford—and there will be many more. It is not our purpose in this chapter to compete with those analyses, nor to attempt to provide a comprehensive review of the coverage. Rather, it is our purpose to place the media coverage of the Iraq war in a broad historical and political context, drawing upon the foundation laid in chapter 2, and to use that context to identify the main themes and, through them, the main flaws in the coverage.

We will not keep you in suspense: We consider the coverage of the Iraq war one of the darkest moments in the history of U.S. journalism. And we consider the deplorable war coverage one of the main factors contributing to the dismal 2004 election coverage. This state of affairs should be appalling not only to those, like us, who opposed the invasion and occupation of Iraq, but also to the invasion's most fervent supporters. Because unless wars are honestly understood, debated, and supported by the population that pays for and fights them and in whose name they are waged they have little or no legitimacy, and they invariably have a cancerous effect upon the body politic. The press is very much in the driver's seat to determine how this scenario plays out. But we see no reason to expect war coverage to improve in the coming years, unless we make fundamental changes in our politics and in our media system.

MANUFACTURING CONSENT FOR WAR

The anti-imperial sentiment of the founders remained popular throughout the first century of the republic's history, although it repeatedly butted up against U.S. expansionism across the North American continent and the de facto domination of much of Latin America. At the beginning of the twentieth century the United States was arguably the strongest economic power in the world, and there was considerable internal pressure for it to assume a military and political role in the world commensurate with its economic status.

Indeed, to much of the political and economic elite of the United States, it was mandatory that the country assume such a role to protect its economic interests. Over time, the idea that the United States needed to embrace the role of global military superpower became a presupposition in the worldview of the U.S. elite, though how it was to be exercised and under what rhetorical banner was subject to occasional loud debate.

Elite belief in the propriety of a globally dominant and militarily aggressive United States was not automatically shared across the population. Many people had difficulty accepting the idea of paying taxes and dying in foreign wars of unclear importance. This is an age-old problem for governments: getting poor and middle-class people to fight and pay for their wars. But in a democracy the problem assumes new dimensions, a higher degree of difficulty. The traditional recourse of simply forcing a nation to go to war and seizing its monies was limited by the ability of people to evict governments through elections and to peacefully organize opposition to wars. In this context, the use of the media as a lever to shape public opinion, to manufacture consent, became a staple insight in political theory, pioneered by Harold Laswell.

Those in power increasingly came to see the battle for domestic public opinion as arguably the single most important front in any prospective war. And another staple insight, though one spoken less loudly, was that telling the truth about the importance of the war from the elite perspective would not necessarily get the job done, since it was assured that the masses were not capable of grasping the importance of war as readily as those in power. To get the masses to line up behind a war, to be willing to die for the cause, generally required some embellishment of the factual record. This also entailed, more often than not, a large dose of flag-waving, nationalism, and, at times, racism. Indeed, Harlan Ullman and James Wade's book, *Shock & Awe,* the 1996 strategic report produced by the U.S. National Defense University on the new age of U.S. warmaking, acknowledged that "Americans prefer not to intervene, especially when the direct threat to the U.S. is ambiguous, tenuous, or difficult to define." Therefore, the authors concluded, it was a practical imperative to have the political cover of U.S. invasions appear to be international efforts. And the media is the institution through which the population must be brought to support invasions.

Again, this is not new. Beginning with the 1898 Spanish-American War, the United States has engaged in scores of foreign military operations and several major wars involving the deployment of U.S. troops. In nearly all of these major wars—the Spanish-American War, World War I, World War II, Korea, Vietnam, the Central America proxy wars of the 1980s, and the first Gulf War—a clear pattern emerged: The President wished to pursue war while the American people had severe reservations. In nearly every case, the White House ran a propaganda campaign to generate public support for going to war, and a campaign that bent the truth in line with the strategy that the ends (war) justified the means (lies). We are not saying that all of these wars by definition were improper. A powerful case, for example, can be made for U.S. participation in World War II. But even in that case, President Roosevelt was concerned that the American people would not fall in line no matter how strong the evidence. So, Roosevelt's critics claimed, he lied us into war.

The news media were placed in a recurring dilemma in each of these wars. Each administration was pursuing aggressive propaganda campaigns to whip up popular support for war, and significant elements, including the leadership, of the party out of power tended to be strongly pro-war. A key battleground for the administration then was winning favorable press coverage. In principle, credible journalism should hold the nation's rulers to the same evidentiary standards it holds the enemies of the nation's rulers. But principle and practice are often at odds. The news media were reportedly presented with the dilemma of either nakedly challenging the administration's pro-war line, demanding hard evidence for claims, digging deep to see that the full story was put before the American people, or going along more or less with the pro-war line. We take no pleasure in reporting that the news media in nearly every case opted for Plan B. In the case of Vietnam, where the Pentagon Papers and the taped sessions in President Johnson's office document the shameless duplicity of the government, the willingness of the news media to parrot administration lies was a thorough abrogation of the requirements of a free press with disastrous consequences for millions of lives. At journalism schools, these episodes are considered embarrassing moments in the history of U.S. journalism and are not dwelled upon in the curricula. (What is dwelled upon is the reporting that challenged official fiction years after the lies were told and the lives were lost.)

On this historical record alone, one would expect that in the future every time a government came forth with a call for war the press corps would ratchet up its skepticism and demand the hardest evidence imaginable before it would participate again in a military adventure. Yet that is never the case. "Look," Dan Rather informed a Harvard forum in July 2004, "when a president of the United States, any president, Republican or Democrat, says these are the facts, there is heavy prejudice, including my own, to give him the benefit of the doubt, and for that I do not apologize."

Rather was wrong. He should have apologized, and that apology should have been directed to the American people, who were misinformed and deceived because of his "heavy prejudice." Similar apologies are due from most of the other mainstream media reporters who covered the preparation for the war in Iraq and its execution. After all, they got almost everything wrong and, more significantly, they fostered false impressions about nonexistent weapons of mass destruction (WMDs) and links between Osama bin Laden and Saddam Hussein that continue to warp the American political discourse.

The explanation for why our news media failed to get the fundamental facts before the American people concerning the decision of whether to go to war in 1917, 1950, 1964, or 2003 are deep-seated. One could argue that the patriotic impulse is such that any journalist will have the strong tendency to root for the home team, as some have put it. But this analysis only begs the question of why the patriotic impulse exists in different forms at different times, why some in society express it more fervently than others, how the patriotic impulse is enforced, how it manifests itself through media institutions and professional practices, and how we explain the exceptions. In short, the patriotic impulse explanation leads to far more questions than it does answers.

To explain the woeful coverage of U.S. wars we return to the crisis in journalism examined in chapter 2. By the early twentieth century, major news media were large commercial organizations and therefore tended to be conservative institutions. Those who owned and managed these firms were, more often than not, comfortable with the worldview of those atop the social structure, because that is where they resided, and supported government policies that were understood to advance those interests. Moreover, most media owners were uncomfortable with being accused of being unpatriotic or treasonous. The system had done well by them. From a structural or sociological perspective, the idea that commercial news media organizations would pose a critical challenge to a strong pro-war campaign is dubious.

But what about the editors and working journalists who composed and edited the news? Some of them proudly hailed from the working class. Certainly they had no such similar allegiance to the policy imperatives of the elite. To the extent they had autonomy from the implicit and explicit institutional prerogatives of the owners, the nature of press coverage was far less certain. Here we could even expect some stubborn interrogation of the powers-that-be. Right? Regrettably, such has only rarely been the case, and to understand this we return to the discussion in chapter 2 of the emergence of professional journalism, which coincided with the emergence of the United States as a global military power. All of the limitations of professional journalism as it developed in the United States—reliance upon official sources, fear of context, and the unstated "dig here, not there" mandate—worked in combination to make professional journalism a lapdog more than a watchdog as the drums of war beat louder.

The factor most scholarship emphasizes in this regard is professional journalism's reliance upon official sources. If people in power are debating an issue, journalists have some wiggle room to root around and explore it. If people in power agree on an issue, presuppose it, or do not seriously debate it, it is almost impossible for a journalist to raise it without being accused of partisanship and pushing an ideological agenda. So it is rarely done, and when it is done it is dismissed as bad journalism.

The ability of official sources to determine the range of legitimate debate is a regrettable tendency for most political stories, but it is nothing short of a disaster for the coverage of the U.S. role in the world. For here ordinary citizens rely to an even greater extent upon the media than they do for domestic politics, where their daily experience can provide something of a corrective to skewed press coverage. Moreover, there is typically a greater consensus among official sources on the benign role of the United States in the world than there is on any other issue, except, perhaps, the greatness of American-style capitalism as the only legitimate way to organize an economy. In short, most news coverage of the role of the United States in the world has a decidedly establishment tenor, and at times constitutes little more than the regurgitation of official perspectives.

This is not to say that there is not highly competent and quality reporting on U.S. foreign policy, only that it tends to stay within the parameters of what official sources consider legitimate. The best reporting, from people like I. F. Stone and Seymour Hersh, goes boldly outside these parameters. (And some of the best reporting on the role of the United States in the world, not surprisingly, comes from reporters working outside the United States, where reliance upon U.S. official sources as the basis for legitimate news and opinion plays a much more limited role.) Sometimes the concerns of dissidents and demonstrators—those outside power—are taken seriously, though in general they are marginalized, trivialized, or ignored. Despite the fact that history reveals that dissidents have often been remarkably accurate in their criticism, as every new war comes along, the skeptics find themselves on the outside of the news cycle looking in.

ARTICLES OF FAITH

Some of the best professional journalism plays off the controversy in foreign affairs policy debates among official sources. But the debates are almost always tactical, i.e., whether an invasion of Vietnam or Panama or Iraq would best serve U.S. interests, not whether it is moral or legal for the United States to invade those nations. The component of the U.S. political elite that was fundamentally hostile to having the United States play the preeminent military role in world affairs has all but disappeared in the past half-century. Those political renegades and Congressional backbenchers who hold such views today are marginalized in the political and media culture. Consider, for example, the treatment of Ohio Representative Dennis Kucinich, a former co-chair of the Congressional Progressive Caucus, or of Texas Republican Ron Paul, a former presidential candidate and one of the few Republicans to openly break with the White House. Both Kucinich and Paul had their facts straight—far straighter than the Bush administration it turned out—and both were prepared to discuss them in engaging detail. Their views reflected those of tens of millions of Americans. Yet, neither man could get on camera during the debate over whether or not to go to war.

There are two fundamental presuppositions—actually, articles of faith—that guide U.S. foreign policy. They are accepted by official sources in both political parties and they are almost never questioned in major U.S. news media.

The first elite presupposition is the notion that the United States is a benevolent force in the world and that whatever it does, by definition, ultimately is about making the world a more just and democratic place. This is a pleasing assumption, and it puts a necessary fig leaf over what may be less altruistic aims. This presupposition makes it possible to dismiss as insignificant anomalies the recurring support for dictators and antidemocratic regimes and the repression of democratic movements that are seen as insufficiently sympathetic to U.S. interests. To cite a few examples: Guatemala and Iran in the 1950s, Brazil, Indonesia, and Greece in the 1960s, Chile and Zaire in the 1970s, El Salvador and Guatemala in the 1980s, Saudi Arabia and Pakistan today.

At an empirical level, if United States foreign policy is driven by a commitment to democracy, it arguably may be among the most incompetently executed policies ever known. The evidence suggests there may be other, less-flattering motivations for U.S. foreign policy, but reporters following the official sources will find little encouragement for critical examination of what these might be. (Perhaps a good place to start would be with criteria used by analysts when assessing the motives of all other powerful nations throughout history: economic self-interest and military pre-eminence.)

This presupposition also makes it possible for there to be almost no debate or discussion of the actual role of the United States in the world. Many Americans accept the official story that the United States is a benevolent giant, attacked on all sides by powerful evildoers. That the United States accounts for almost half of all military spending in the world; that U.S. military spending dwarfs the second largest military power by a factor of eight; that the United States has hundreds of foreign military bases in literally scores of nations, whereas hardly any other country in the world has a single military base outside its own borders: All of this is largely unmentioned and unknown to Americans. It is simply assumed away. And that leaves most Americans largely clueless about how the United States is perceived in the rest of the world.

The second elite presupposition that is unquestioned in U.S. media coverage of U.S. foreign affairs is the notion that the United States, and the United States alone, has a 007-like right to invade any country it wishes. The United States also reserves the right to "deputize" an ally to conduct an invasion if it so desires, but otherwise other nations are not permitted to engage in the invasion business. This presents a small problem for the political elite and for the news media. After all, the UN charter and a number of other treaties signed by the United States prohibit the invasion of one nation by another unless it is under armed attack. Moreover, the U.S. Constitution characterizes treaties as the highest law of the land, so that if the United States violates international law, it arguably warrants presidential impeachment. To top it off, in popular discourse, the United States proudly promotes itself as favoring the rule of law, and a main argument against all of its adversaries is invariably that they are liars who ignore treaties they have signed. That is, in fact, sometimes used as a rationale for a U.S. invasion.

The problem the United States faces is that almost all of its invasions violate international law, and sometimes, as in the case of Iraq, in a blatant manner. So how do the political elite and the news media reconcile this contradiction? Simple: They ignore it. It is virtually unthinkable for a mainstream U.S. reporter to even pursue this issue. When the United States invaded Panama in 1990—three or four invasions ago for those of you keeping score at home—then Secretary of State James Baker held a press conference on the issue. Near the end, he called on a reporter who happened to be from a small outlet.

She mentioned that the U.S. invasion violated the charter of the Organization of American States to which both Panama and the United States were signatories, and that the U.S. Constitution regarded treaties like the OAS charter as the highest law of the land. She asked Secretary Baker his thoughts. The generally unflappable Baker seemed nearly speechless—no American official had been asked such a question by a reporter in years—until he muttered something to the effect that his lawyers would look into it. The matter was never raised again.

Let us be clear about this. We are not saying categorically the United States should not violate international law and pursue invasions in a manner that we would condemn other nations for pursuing. Nor are we saying that international law should not be changed. We have seen in elite circles serious arguments put forth to make that case. Our point is that if it is a worthy point of discussion for elites behind closed doors, if illegal invasions are a justifiable practice, credible journalism would make it a point worthy of evaluation and debate for the citizenry. It would not participate in the obfuscation of such a central legal and moral issue. Our own hunch is that the American people would not go along with invasions so willingly if the issue were understood in this manner. Those in power recognize this and therefore have very little incentive to raise this issue before the public.

In combination, the limitations of professional journalism, the influence of owners, the linkages of media institutions to the power structure of society, and the internalized presuppositions, have led to what can only be characterized as a palpable double standard in coverage of the U.S. role in the world. None have demonstrated this more convincingly than Edward S. Herman and Noam Chomsky in their book, *Manufacturing Consent*. Stories that support the aims of U.S. policymakers get lavish and sympathetic treatment; stories of similar or greater factual veracity and importance that undermine U.S. policy goals get brief and unfavorable mention. As Howard Friel and Richard Falk have demonstrated in their research, the U.S. news media, including our most respected newspapers like the *New York Times,* turn a blind eye to U.S. violations of core international law, while having no qualms about playing up the violations of adversaries. It would be nearly impossible for the coverage to be more unprincipled.

THE CONTEMPORARY CRISIS IN JOURNALISM

The problems with U.S. media coverage described above were evident from the 1960s into the 1980s, the so-called golden age of professional journalism. Press coverage exhibited severe flaws even when the newsrooms were relatively flush with resources and had as much autonomy as they ever would. The main developments in journalism over the past two decades that have eroded professional journalism have only made the situation worse.

The corporate downsizing and cutback epidemic has been especially hard on international coverage, as we discussed in chapter 2. The sharp reduction in the number of foreign correspondents working for U.S. news media has been a familiar story over the past two decades. These are positions that cost a lot of money and to the managers in charge they don't seem to generate any black ink. Moreover, managers argue that people don't seem to care if there is less international coverage, or if what passes for international coverage has less to do with politics and more to do with easy-to-report natural disasters and plane crashes. So from the corporate worldview, axing these positions is a no-brainer.

The problem with not having many foreign correspondents with a familiarity with the language, history, and customs of the regions they were covering has become painfully clear over the past fifteen years. When conflicts break out in the Balkans, Africa, South Asia, or elsewhere, U.S. news media have few if any reporters on the ground to provide context for the story. What this means is that there is less capacity for journalists to provide a counterbalance to whatever official story Washington puts forward. At its worst, foreign reporting becomes celebrity journalists and anchors airdropped into a crisis area and shepherded around by representatives of the U.S. government. This is not the recipe for independent journalism.

The other core attack on professional journalism—the right-wing critique of the "liberal" media—has not helped matters either. Antiwar criticism of a Democratic warmaker from the Right, though rare, is kosher if framed in hypernationalist terms—Sean Hannity attacked Clinton's Kosovo war in terms he characterized as treasonous when he debated later with others about President Bush's Iraq war. An incessant aspect of the right-wing critique of the "liberal" news media is that journalists are insufficiently patriotic; this translates into journalists being extrasensitive to prove their nationalist credentials. Again, this is not conducive to critical analysis of foreign wars.

The combined effect of commercial and conservative attacks on professional journalism is to undermine the formal adherence to a neutral and nonpartisan position by the news media. This does not mean mainstream media can become explicitly partisan on the left; that is more unthinkable than ever. Nor does it mean that most news media have dropped their formal commitment to political neutrality. But it does mean there are a growing number of media that see themselves as pushing a partisan pro-Republican political agenda, often under a thin veneer of being "fair and balanced." The veneer is there for show purposes. So it is that the FOX News Channel, Sinclair Broadcasting, the *New York Post,* the *Washington Times,* the editorial page of the *Wall Street Journal,* most of talk radio, all serve as couriers for the Republican Right. They aggressively promote right-wing policies and bash Democrats who get in the way. In coverage of Republican wars this translates into aggressive pro-war posturing and wholesale rabid condemnation of antiwar criticism as unpatriotic or treasonous. Because the rest of the news media tend to be timid by comparison, this right-wing phalanx sets the tone for coverage out of proportion to its actual size. And the rest of the press becomes even more hesitant to contradict the government line.

Changes for the worse in journalism have been aggravated by a more aggressive determination by the government to control the news concerning war. If the lesson of Vietnam for activists and scholars was that the press was a conduit for government lies, for those in the White House and the military the lesson was that the press needed to have an even shorter leash. The relative freedom reporters had to travel around Vietnam during the war in that country was regarded as a central factor in fomenting antiwar attitudes at home as the war dragged on. Indeed, elements of the military blame the defeat in Vietnam on press coverage that undermined public support for what was originally seen as a justifiable war. The solution was not to stop engaging in such wars, but to change the manner in which the media covered the wars. Each subsequent administration has devoted ever more attention to controlling the news of war.

No government has approached controlling the news with the aggressiveness of the current Bush administration. Despite its rhetoric about small government, ethics and transparency, the Bush administration has made it clear that the less the people know about what the government is doing the better. As Eric Alterman chronicles, open-record laws nationwide have been rolled back three hundred times during the Bush tenure and the pace of classification of federal government documents has shot up 75 percent. Attorney General John Ashcroft relaxed the basis for fulfilling Freedom of Information Act (FOIA) requests by citizens, and the Bush administration has moved to stonewall all efforts to put public light on their activities. "It's become much, much harder to get responses to FOIA requests, and it's taking much, much longer," Alterman quotes one lawyer working with the Associated Press as saying. "Agencies seem to view their role as coming up with techniques to keep information secret rather than the other way around. That is completely contrary to the goal of the act."

The Bush administration has worked to undermine the independence of the press in more direct ways as well. From the beginning of his first term, George W. Bush held few press conferences. Then, to lessen the degree of difficulty for the president, the Bush administration admitted a partisan right-wing impostor with no journalistic credentials—Jeff Gannon, aka Jeff Guckert—to a scarce slot in the White House press corps to lob softball questions on those occasions when the president did meet the press. Gannon's experience for his public duty apparently had been operating an on-line gay escort service. One can only imagine how the right-wing punditocracy would have responded had Bill Clinton pulled a maneuver like this—a rumor about Clinton getting an expensive haircut on an airport tarmac drove them to the edge of sanity—but to the Limbaughs and Hannitys of the world, the Gannon/Guckert affair was entirely uninteresting.

Even more striking was the revelation that the Bush administration covertly paid journalists to help promote its policies. Armstrong

Williams received $240,000 to pump up the White House's education policies under the guise of being a credible journalist. Two other reporters, Michael McManus and Maggie Gallagher, were also paid under the table to do the White House bidding. Gallagher received less than Williams, prompting Kim Gandy of the National Organization for Women to crack, "Women not only can't get equal pay, we can't get equal payola."

Last but not least, some twenty federal agencies, under Bush administration directives, financed the production of video news releases promoting administration policies, which were submitted to commercial TV stations where they were sometimes broadcast as legitimate news without any disclaimer. The budget for all these secret propaganda activities runs in the range of $250 million, an amount equaling two-thirds of the entire federal budget for public radio and television. In all of the above examples, the Bush administration has stonewalled efforts to get to the truth, and has used Republican control of Congress to prevent an independent investigation. In short, it is an administration with contempt for the principles of a free press. And in the matter of war, where the importance of media is front and center, the Bush administration propaganda campaign has been at full throttle.

9/11 AND THE WAR ON TERROR

All of these factors came together in the coverage of the terrorist attacks of September 11, 2001, and the subsequent invasion and occupation of Afghanistan. Despite the massive amount of attention the news media devoted to the topic—it was arguably the biggest U.S. news story in a half-century—coverage was heavily propagandistic. Elementary examinations of the administration's performance in failing to prevent the attack were not pursued. Hard looks at the relationship between the Bush administration and previous U.S. governments with Mideast governments and terrorist activities, including

those of al Qaeda, were all but nonexistent. Even to broach the logical question of why the terrorists attacked the United States—as if there might be a rational explanation beyond the idea that these were madmen who hated us because of our freedoms—was dismissed as implicitly condoning the attack and mass murder.

Guided by the Bush administration and official sources, these terrorist acts were converted within hours of 9/11 from vicious crimes against humanity to acts of war. The former route to capturing global criminals employed existing treaties and global law enforcement to search out the guilty parties and bring them to justice. (As journalist

Tom Engelhardt demonstrates, nearly all of the success that has come since 9/11 in capturing terrorists and infiltrating terrorist networks has come precisely through this course of action.) The new route, the declaration of a war on terror, was a radical response by the Bush administration and U.S. policy elites and ordained by the news media. Few issues have been less debated and less debatable in recent U.S. political life.

The war on terrorism entailed a push for a broad militarization of society and, immediately, for the invasion and bombing of Afghanistan, a nation that did not attack the United States on 9/11. That there might be another explanation for the invasion and occupation of Afghanistan was unthinkable. Once the heroic invasion was completed, it all but dropped off the U.S. news map. Few Americans have any idea of the conditions in that country today except that it is now an "emerging democracy," because our president tells us so. In fact, Afghanistan is a colossal mess, in the midst of ongoing warfare and chaos, where terrorism is as strong as ever, and has now joined the front ranks of the world's leading narco-states. Of course Osama bin Laden and the leadership of al Qaeda and the Taliban, the bad guys we were going to smoke out of the caves, remain mostly at large. To the extent we have caught any of them, it has come through conventional law enforcement.

The turn to a war on terror also gave the green light to an even-more secretive Bush administration—after all, this is World War III—and one with even greater contempt for press efforts to illuminate government operations for the public. It meant that the United States became even more aggressive in surreptitiously spreading its propaganda—there is no more accurate word in the English language—to media around the world. The Pentagon even established an Office of Strategic Influence following 9/11 to plant false news stories in foreign media. When the public caught wind of it, the government was forced to close the office, but the government concedes the work continues under other auspices. As mentioned above, the Bush administration has understandably brought this same contempt for public information to the home front, which, after all, is the most important front in modern war. Somewhere near Orange, Virginia, if one puts one's ear close to the ground, one can hear the sound of Madison turning over in his grave.

The truth about 9/11 is still largely unknown. But what pieces that have emerged, mostly in the margins and with all-too-little pressure from mainstream media, suggest that much of what was presented as received wisdom in the months following the 9/11 attacks was incorrect, if not nonsense. The testimony of Richard Clarke as well as the report of the 9/11 Commission both highlight the negligence of the administration's conduct in failing to stop the terrorist attack or in addressing it properly afterward. One can only imagine what mainstream media, egged on by FOX News, the *Wall Street Journal* editorial page, talk radio, and the *New York Post,* would have done to a President Gore or a President Clinton in a similar situation. In the immediate aftermath of the 9/11 attacks, courtesy of a hyperventilating press, President Bush was reborn as a cross between Abraham Lincoln and Winston Churchill.

Ironically, the general consensus of press observers in the aftermath of 9/11 was that the mainstream press had hit a 560-foot home run over the centerfield wall. Backslapping abounded. Dan Gillmor presented a common perspective when he wrote, "Journalists did some of their finest work and made me proud to be one of them." And Gillmor was correct, in a narrow sense. There was around-the-clock coverage and high technology to keep us on top of what people in power were saying and how people in the nation were responding. It was at times extraordinary and often dazzling, and it brought us together. But the immediacy and drama of the coverage of the 9/11 attacks and the immediately ordained war on terror also meant that elementary questioning and investigation of Bush administration conduct and policy initiatives were largely missing. In a climate where the political Right was bloviating on the flames of blind nationalism, to even raise a tough question was unpatriotic, if not treasonous. In retrospect, much of the content of the mainstream press would have been compatible with the output of a kept press system in an authoritarian regime.

Prominent right-wing pundit Peggy Noonan, who invariably promoted the Bush administration without a shred of doubt, actually praised the media coverage following 9/11 as exemplary. Conservative media watch groups were so ecstatic that they even hailed Dan Rather, a man who historically had topped their hit list. The press was eating out of the Bush administration's bowl. If media truly constituted the most important front in modern war, the stars were in alignment for a bold invasion that had been atop the wish list of Bush foreign policy advisors for years, but was once thought too politically controversial to accomplish: the invasion of Iraq.

BUILDUP TO THE INVASION OF IRAQ

It was in this environment that the United States was able to launch an invasion and occupation of Iraq on entirely bogus grounds. The three major justifications offered explicitly and implicitly by the Bush administration to generate public support for the war were: 1) that Iraq illegally possessed weapons of mass destruction and was poised to use them on the United States in the immediate future; 2) that Iraq had been somehow connected to the attacks on 9/11, so pursuing Saddam Hussein was a rational next step in the campaign against bin Laden; and 3) Iraq was the leading terrorist state, 9/11 notwithstanding, so the war on terror had to go through Baghdad.

The second and third claims were unsubstantiated on their face, and borderline preposterous. The Bush administration was careful about making these claims in any official setting, but utterly shameless about turning to these claims to win support on the home front. President Bush, Secretary of State Colin Powell, and Vice President Dick Cheney invoked these themes in their speeches. Cheney said, "Iraq is now the central front in the war on terror." This assertion begged the question that if it is justifiable to overthrow a government because it is supportive in some manner to global terror networks, would Iraq be atop the list? By some intelligence assessments, other non-democratic governments had much closer links to al Qaeda than Iraq. But these were U.S. allies like Pakistan and Saudi Arabia, and the matter was almost never raised. The news media instead routinely reinforced the Bush administration propaganda goal of linking Iraq to 9/11 and the war on terror, generally framing coverage of Iraq in terms of being part of this war. FOX News took the lead, placing the urgent heading WAR ON TERROR on the screen whenever news concerning Iraq was being presented.

The irony is that Islamist terrorist networks arguably are now vastly stronger as a result of the U.S. invasion of Iraq. Recruitment is up, as the U.S. invasion confirms the Islamists' critique of the United States as an Arab-hating imperialist power. Iraq, once a secular nation frowned upon by Muslim fundamentalists, now teems with terrorist activity. Indeed, as Paul Krugman notes, a CIA classified report in the summer of 2005 reached exactly this conclusion: "Iraq has become what Afghanistan was under Soviet occupation, only more so: a magnet and training ground for Islamic extremists, who will eventually threaten other countries." This point contradicted the media framing *in toto* and was pushed to the margins of polite discourse.

The legal case the United States made for a pre-emptive invasion of Iraq was the issue of Iraq's possession of weapons of mass destruction capable of being used against the United States. This case was made with considerable fanfare, both for domestic audiences and to generate global support. It, too, was dubious, with significant evidence undermining its credibility. As is now established beyond any and all doubt: There were no weapons of mass destruction in Iraq. The Bush administration pushed its claims with little concern for evidence, and the news media participated in this fraud to an appalling extent. (The May 2005 disclosure of the pre-invasion British intelligence "Downing Street memo" that provided damning evidence about how the United States was cooking intelligence to justify the invasion of Iraq—the "smoking gun memo"—was the final nail in a well-shut coffin.) This episode has been diagnosed in detail and is now considered one of the darkest moments in the entire history of U.S. journalism.

Lost, too, in the coverage was the unalterable fact that the U.S. invasion of Iraq violated international law.

All of the factors highlighted in chapter 2 and above explain this dreadful media coverage. In addition, the media institutions themselves were hawkish. The *Columbia Journalism Review* reviewed the editorial pages of the top six dailies that influence public opinion, including the *New York Times, Washington Post, Wall Street Journal,* and *USA Today,* and determined that all of them failed to hold the Bush administration to an adequate standard for proof. *Editor & Publisher* found that of the top fifty daily newspapers in the nation, not a single one was strongly antiwar on its editorial page.

The reliance upon official sources to frame the debate and set the agenda is mostly responsible for the disgraceful press coverage of Bush administration lies. As Jonathan Mermin put it in a brilliant essay in *World Policy Journal,* conventional journalistic practice means "journalists continue to be incapable of focusing on an issue for perspective on U.S. foreign policy that has not been first identified or articulated in official Washington debate." Here it is important to note that most Democratic leaders did not assume an antiwar position, so there was little countervailing framing coming from officialdom. Mermin scoffs at the idea that elite consensus justifies journalists regurgitating the government position uncritically: "The absence of opposition to a Republican military intervention among Democratic politicians is not persuasive evidence that the policy is sound, or even that presumptively informed and thoughtful people believe it sound." What it adds up to, in clear contradiction to the spirit and intent of the First Amendment, is "if the government isn't talking about it, we don't report it."

A comprehensive analysis of the sources used on TV news in the weeks leading up to the U.S. invasion—when a significant percentage of the U.S. population was opposed to an invasion—showed that 3 percent of the sources employed were antiwar and over 70 percent were decidedly pro-war. A Fairness & Accuracy in Reporting (FAIR) survey of nightly news coverage on NBC, ABC, CBS, PBS, CNN, and FOX during the first three weeks after the invasion found that pro-war U.S. sources outnumbered antiwar sources by twenty-five to one. Moreover, the on-air experts that TV news relied upon generally were establishment figures and by nature uncritical.

Press coverage reached its nadir, its Death Valley, in two public events immediately preceding the invasion. In February 2003, Colin Powell went before the United Nations to make the definitive case for invading Iraq. Powell provided little verifiable evidence for his extravagant claims. Six months later, Associated Press correspondent Charles J. Hanley fact-checked Powell's speech, and "utterly demolished" it, as *Editor & Publisher* put it. Regrettably, our best journalism all too often tends to be in postmortems, when the political consequences are minuscule. At the time of Powell's speech, when the fate of a war hung in the balance and when independent experts were puncturing most of his claims, the news media regurgitated Powell's points and praised them for their veracity in a manner that could not have been exceeded by Stalin's stooges. Gilbert Cranberg, formerly of the *Des Moines Register,* compiled a comprehensive study of the press coverage of Powell's speech. Among the terms used by our leading papers (as listed by Eric Alterman in April 2005 in *The Nation*) to describe the merits of Powell's case: "a massive array of evidence"; "a sober, factual case"; "an overwhelming case"; "a smoking fusillade . . . a persuasive case for anyone who is still persuadable"; "an ironclad case . . . incontrovertible evidence"; "an accumulation of painstakingly gathered and analyzed evidence"; "succinct and damning evidence . . . the case is closed."

If the abdication of any notion of elementary journalism in the coverage of Powell's UN speech was tragic, the press conduct at Bush's last prewar press conference was a farce. In its one opportunity to grill the president about his case for war, there was a striking lack of hard or pointed questioning as we discussed in chapter 1. The White House press corps looked more like court reporters than journalists.

In past wars like Vietnam, apologists for gullible press coverage could argue that the news media had no way of knowing that the Johnson administration was lying to them, and that the Gulf of Tonkin incident was a ruse. Such was not the case with Iraq. Every step of the way, there was an impressive amount of material in the international press and on the Internet that contradicted the Bush administration's line. (For example, consider the powerful and immediate rebuttal to Powell's UN speech by Glen Rangwala of Cambridge University.) It was all but ignored. Former marine and United Nations weapons inspector Scott Ritter—who spent years on the ground in Iraq—carefully repudiated all of the Bush administration claims; as a result he was subject to a character assassination campaign that made it easier for a news medium to turn to Lee Greenwood, Chuck Norris, or Mike Ditka as a credible expert. A journalist did not have to be I. F. Stone to see that there was something fishy about the official story; all she had to do was keep her eyes open and her critical faculties working.

Moreover, unlike Vietnam, the invasion of Iraq was met by a massive antiwar movement in the United States *before* any bullets were expended. Hundreds of thousands of Americans took to the streets in February 2003 to protest the planned invasion of Iraq. Press coverage, following the familiar pattern for dissident opinion, was minimal and dismissive. (By comparison, a relative handful of protesters outside of Terry Schiavo's hospital in March 2005, enunciating the opinions of the Republican leadership, were accorded lavish and respectful coverage by the media.) One of the striking developments of recent times has been the increasing difficulty of assembled dissident citizens to gain press coverage and to influence public opinion. In addition, protesters are increasingly shunted into far corners of cities to what are termed with no sense of irony "Free Speech Zones" to do their demonstrating in such a way that no one in power or the general public will have to pay any attention to them. Regrettably, major media have done too little to challenge this development.

Mainstream journalists should be less dismissive of those outside of power who wish to exercise opinions on whether to go to war. The antiwar critique has been proven far more accurate than that of the Bush administration. It is an apt reminder for why "the right of the people peaceably to assemble, and to petition the government for a redress of grievances" is inscribed in the First Amendment, and why we should be concerned about its banishment to free speech zones. But don't hold your breath. It certainly doesn't help matters that the "parent companies of the media are becoming increasingly reluctant to go out on a limb about anything controversial," as Elizabeth Guider put it in *Variety*. "The corporate agendas of these mini-nation-states," she continued, "have become so complex and politically sensitized that anything perceived as out of the mainstream is automatically viewed by top brass with suspicion."

MANAGING THE HOME FRONT DURING WAR

Perhaps the most striking development in press coverage of the invasion and war was the policy of embedding journalists with military units, so they could see first-hand how the war was developing. Proponents of the policy argued it would protect journalists from enemy fire and make it possible for them to get stories that would be otherwise unattainable. "During this time of war, the images over our televisions, the sounds over our radios, the ink on our newsprint and the words and images over the Internet are testaments to many of the core values of our great nation and any true open democracy," the thrilled Michael Powell told the Media Institute less than ten days after the invasion began. "Indeed," he continued, "by embedding over five hundred reporters around the world with military units, we are seeing a degree of media coverage never before experienced in any previous war. The real-time pictures and reports are a result of remarkable developments in communications technology and the breadth of media platforms." James L. Gattuso, a research fellow with the conservative Heritage Foundation, suggested that the coverage of the war ought to convince Powell and his fellow FCC members that all was well with the media: "The debate will be filled with endless factoids and pleadings. But . . . when the commissioners finally sit down to assess the media marketplace, they will remember these days in March, and the cornucopia of information and perspectives that the market provided."

More sober observers saw things differently. Veteran journalist Studs Terkel said "embedded sounds an awful lot like 'in bed with' to me." Terkel and others complained that "embedded" journalists worked for the most part under the control of the military and made little effort to provide independent coverage. The combination of embedded reporters on the ground in Iraq with military experts in the TV studios of Washington and New York meant that press coverage concentrated narrowly upon the tactics of war from a purely U.S. perspective. And, as Michael Massing notes, those embedded reporters who wrote negatively about the military found themselves blacklisted. Moreover, to be an unembedded journalist in Iraq was a very risky proposition, and the death rate for journalists was striking from both Iraqi insurgents and U.S. military forces alike. If you were not embedded, there was a good chance that you would be someone's target.

Embedded reporting in combination with full-throttle jingoism on U.S. television news made it difficult for journalists to do critical work. "Nobody wants to be too much of a pain in the ass in a newspaper," explained Seymour Hersh, the Pulitzer Prize–winning journalist. "And if you keep pushing the envelope you'll get in trouble." BBC Director General Greg Dyke, whose home country, Great Britain, was the main U.S. ally in the war, admitted in April 2003, that he was "shocked while in the United States by how unquestioning the broadcast news was during the war." Some leading U.S. broadcast news reporters shared Dyke's disgust. "It was a grand and glorious picture that had a lot of people watching and a lot of advertisers excited about cable TV news," MSNBC's Ashleigh Banfield announced in April 2003. "But it wasn't journalism." "I think the press was muzzled, and I think the press was self-muzzled," stated CNN's Christine Amanpour, arguably the most respected foreign correspondent on U.S. television, a few months later. "I'm sorry to say, but certainly television and, perhaps, to a certain extent, my station was intimidated by the administration and its foot soldiers at FOX News. And it did, in fact, put a climate of fear and self-censorship, in my view, in terms of the kind of broadcast work we did."

The problems continued after the formal defeat of Saddam Hussein's army during the liberation that became an occupation. The U.S. news media were caught entirely by surprise. Indeed, the term "occupation" had never been used prior to the invasion. Mermin quotes PBS's Jim Lehrer, who defended this omission: "The word occupation . . . was never mentioned in the run-up to the war. It was liberation. This was [talked about in Washington as] a war of liberation, not a war of occupation. So as a consequence, those of us in journalism never even looked at the issue of occupation."

The uprising and opposition to the U.S. presence, which illustrated the lack of enthusiasm for the U.S. "liberation" of Iraq, gnawed at the narrative being promoted in U.S. news reports. Analyst Jonathan Schell and others have argued that the situation was similar to Vietnam, and reporters were ill-equipped to understand a "liberation" invasion that is not popularly embraced by those being liberated. Nir Rosen, an American freelance reporter in Iraq who is fluent in Arabic, told Massing that, as might be expected from an occupying army facing a guerrilla war, American soldiers tended to "treat everybody as the enemy." Moreover, U.S. allies included some of the sleazier and more corrupt opportunists in Iraq. When nine billion dollars being held by the U.S. hand-picked interim government disappeared, it suggested deep-seated problems of legitimacy, a la Vietnam. Understood in this manner, the torture scandal of Abu Ghraib prison was not an anomaly, but more or less what one might expect.

At the same time, it was imperative for the Bush administration that the best possible spin be put on the war, that it be regarded as a success on the home front, especially with an election coming up. The one great advantage the Bush administration had was that it could use its power to heavily promote stories that painted the picture it wanted to be seen, and by remaining quiet it could pour water on those stories it did not wish to see developed. When information continued to emerge discrediting the Bush administration's rationale for the war and the nature of the "liberation" like the "Downing Street memo" from Britain, the White House sealed its lips, Democrats meekly obliged, and reporters seemingly had little to work with. As a result journalistic mountains were converted into molehills.

Conversely, stories like the toppling of the Saddam Hussein statue in Baghdad, President Bush dressing up in flight-suit drag and appearing before a giant MISSION ACCOMPLISHED banner, the rescue of Jessica Lynch, the capture of Saddam Hussein, and the Iraqi election of early 2005 all got lavish attention at the time such attention was needed. Each of these was held up as a critical juncture, the moment the tide was turning and the Bush administration's policies were being proven right.

But, in each instance, the passage of only a few days or weeks would reveal that the tide had not turned and that the administration's approach remained as ill-fated as ever.

Consider the torture scandal at Abu Ghraib prison. Award-winning Associated Press reporter Charles Hanley broke a story on U.S. torture of Iraqi prisoners in the fall of 2003, but, as Mermin notes, it "was ignored by the major American newspapers." Hanley explained that his "was not an officially sanctioned story that begins with a handout from an official source." There is a "very strong prejudice," Hanley told Mermin, "toward investing U.S. official statements with credibility while disregarding statements from almost any other source," such as (in Hanley's story) Iraqis recounting their personal experiences at Abu Ghraib. Hanley's story did not provoke a Bush photo-op in a warden's costume in front of Abu Ghraib, or a steady stream of official press releases drawing attention to it. When it finally was broken with photographic evidence by Hersh and CBS News in the U.S., the story received plentiful coverage. But it was a classic case in which the line of investigation stopped at low levels, and exonerated those in charge of the overall policy. Without getting any push from official sources, the story faded away. Indeed, it went largely unmentioned during the 2004 presidential campaign debates.

One year after the Abu Ghraib story broke, Seymour Hersh reflected on the whitewash of extensive and persistent U.S. war crimes, which he among others has documented, and the role the U.S. media played. "It's a dreary pattern," Hersh wrote. "The reports and subsequent Senate proceedings are sometimes criticized on editorial pages. There are calls for a truly independent investigation by the Senate or the House. Then, as months pass with no official action, the issue withers away, until the next set of revelations revives it." There were ten official military inquiries into Abu Ghraib, but they "are all asking the wrong questions . . . The question that never gets adequately answered is this: What did the president do after being told about Abu Ghraib?"

(Absurdly, far more U.S. media intensity was applied to *Newsweek* magazine in May 2005 when it was revealed that *Newsweek*'s sourcing for a claim that the military had flushed a Koran down the toilet during prisoner interrogation was flawed. The White House and the right-wing echo chamber jumped on this story with a savage fury and it managed to do the impossible: push Michael Jackson and the Runaway Bride out of the headlines. Soon the entirety of the news media was engulfed in the story. The White House and the Right intimated that this technicality—because evidence suggested that sourcing aside, it was probably true; and anyway flushing a Koran was mild compared to the extensive abuse of prisoners already well documented, though thinly reported—demonstrated the "liberal" media had an antiwar axe to grind, and all coverage critical of the war should be dismissed as propaganda. Ironically, or more accurately, tragically, at the same time as the *Newsweek* scandal, the U.S. news media all but ignored the "Downing Street memo" that established that the Bush administration fixed intelligence to get public support for the invasion of Iraq. The U.S. press likewise gave short shrift to an Amnesty International report released on April 26, 2005, strongly criticizing the United States for its treatment of prisoners of war, and characterizing the U.S. prison at Guantanamo Bay as a "gulag." The Bush administration dismissed the charges as absurd and the U.S. media obediently dropped the story, leaving it to Amnesty International to remind journalists that the Bush Administration routinely cited Amnesty International findings as clinching evidence when making its case against North Korea or Cuba or Saddam Hussein. The Downing Street memo and the Amnesty International report, apparently, were small potatoes compared to *Newsweek*'s "crime.")

To put the Abu Ghraib coverage in context, imagine for a second that the shoe was on the other foot. Imagine that Saddam Hussein's forces had captured Americans and subjected them to grotesque humiliation and outright torture in April 2003. Imagine if Saddam Hussein claimed he had no personal knowledge and the problem lay with some overzealous troops. He said he was sorry about it, but, hey, it was a one-time mix-up and would never happen again. Imagine there was evidence suggesting it was more widespread than the first wave of evidence confirmed, and that Bibles had been desecrated. Would this story have faded away so quickly? Would Saddam Hussein's excuse have been accepted by the U.S. press as plausible, and the matter largely dropped? Or would it have been like a new Twin Towers demolition on the American consciousness? These are rhetorical questions because we know the answers.

A major area where the tension between the goals of the Bush administration to paint the rosiest picture possible and the role of reporters to present a more accurate picture of what is transpiring in Iraq surrounds the reporting of the war's toll on human lives. The U.S. government wishes to minimize the public's recognition of the human cost of war both to the Iraqis and to U.S. soldiers. Wary of

Vietnam-like images, the Bush administration fought to keep this information strictly outside of public view. Iraqi casualties were not recorded, and reporters have been unable to get to the places where most of these casualties occur. As a result, Massing notes, journalists have been "exceedingly cautious" in making estimates. While few U.S. journalists had any interest in this subject, the respected British medical journal *The Lancet* published a study by Johns Hopkins University scholars who estimated the Iraqi civilian death toll at 100,000 in October 2004, before the second siege of Fallujah, with a majority of the deaths due to U.S. military actions. The report was controversial, and subject to legitimate dispute from other experts who believe it exaggerated the death toll, but the entire matter died quickly enough in the U.S. press, as no official U.S. source wished to dwell on this topic. This lack of interest in keeping an accurate accounting of Iraqi civilian deaths tends to undermine the official claim that this war is motivated by a great concern for the welfare of the Iraqi people.

"The vast amount of suffering and death endured by civilians as a result of the U.S.-led invasion of Iraq has, for the most part, been carefully kept out of the consciousness of the average American," Bob Herbert noted in April 2005. "As for the press, it has better things to cover than the suffering of civilians in war. The aversion to this topic is at the opposite extreme from the ecstatic journalistic embrace of the death of one pope and the election of another, and the media's manic obsession with the comings and goings of Martha, Jacko, et al."

The matter of U.S. casualties is even more striking, as there is a clear interest in this subject on the home front. On the one hand, as *Editor & Publisher* reported in November 2004, the Bush administration has been revealed to "routinely undercount" U.S. casualties, especially of those soldiers and pilots seriously injured but not killed. On the other hand, following a policy put in place by the first President Bush, the press was barred from covering the arrival of caskets at Dover Air Force Base in Delaware. To insure the success of this policy, soldiers' corpses were flown to the United States in the dead of night. When Ted Koppel's *Nightline* devoted an entire program to honor the dead soldiers by simply reading their names and showing their pictures over the air, Koppel was accused of being unpatriotic, and several ABC affiliates, in particular those owned by the Sinclair chain, refused to carry the program. One of the few major U.S. newspapers willing to violate the government's ban was the independently owned *Seattle Times,* which alone showed photographs of the returning dead soldiers on its front page.

The message has been sent explicitly and implicitly that the U.S. government does not want the American people to see the human cost of this war, and our media, with only a handful of exceptions, has obliged. The government said "jump." And the media responded "how high?"

MEDIA MOMENT OF TRUTH

Although U.S. journalism, especially in coverage of wars, tends to run in packs, it is not monolithic. Even at its worst there is usually an exception that proves the rule. In addition, among the ranks of journalists are many highly principled and courageous reporters, who entered the profession not to serve as a conduit for powerful elites, but to shine a light on those in power on behalf of the citizenry. As the dissonance grew between the official story offered by the White House with the actual horror story on the ground in Iraq, many journalists took a hard look at media performance and the state of the profession. By the end of 2003, the *Columbia Journalism Review, Editor & Publisher,* and other leading industry publications or journalism reviews—not to mention the first-rate work done by groups like FAIR and publications like the *New York Review of Books* and *The Nation*—had presented probing criticism of media coverage of the war. Much of the material in this chapter draws from that work.

In early 2004, the *New York Times* made the unprecedented gesture of offering a mea culpa for its flawed coverage of the weapons of mass destruction controversy, while the *Washington Post* allowed its media reporter, Howard Kurtz, to write an extended critique of its coverage. Each newspaper implicitly acknowledged their role in leading the nation to war on bogus grounds, yet neither explicitly took responsibility. The confessions were halting and unenthusiastic, but, in a field where admissions of fundamental errors are about as welcome as getting root canal surgery without a painkiller, they sent a powerful shot over the bow of journalism nationwide. This occurred on the heels of Howard Dean's rise to the top of the Democratic field running on an essentially antiwar platform, and as observers were beginning to use words like "quagmire" to describe the U.S. occupation of Iraq. The apologias were the tip of the journalistic iceberg. Many journalists were appalled by the war, humiliated by the poor performance of the news media, and frustrated by the Bush administration's deception. Some critics predicted that the working press would get a wake-up call from the scandalous coverage of the Iraq war and turn its anger on Bush in advance of the November election. If there was going to be room for more independent and critical coverage of the U.S. war on Iraq, conditions were as ripe as ever in newsrooms in early 2004.

Alas, it would not come to pass. The impulse for media self-criticism is quickly tempered by the deeply ingrained institutional realization that it is not healthy to encourage the public to keep the hood up any longer than necessary so they can inspect the engine. Few other major media took the bait and pursued the issue of how the media were complicit in sponsoring a devastating and illegitimate war. It was left to a columnist for a small paper in Fredericksburg, Virginia, to forthrightly apologize to the American public on behalf of the news media. "Sorry we let unsubstantiated claims drive our coverage. Sorry we were dismissive of experts who disputed the White House charges against Iraq," Rick Mercier wrote on the first anniversary of the invasion in March 2004. "Sorry we let a band of self-serving Iraqi defectors make fools of us. Sorry we fell for Colin Powell's performance at the United Nations. Sorry we couldn't hold the administration's feet to the fire when it really mattered." Mercier conceded it was "absurd to receive this apology from a person so low in the media hierarchy," but that was the best the public would get. It was difficult to avoid Danny Schechter's conclusion that the mainstream press made minimum concessions on its Iraq coverage as a form of damage control; there was no interest in laying out the whole truth.

The *New York Times* certainly wanted to get the incident in its rearview mirror as quickly as possible. The *Times* quietly removed Judith Miller—the reporter whose uncritical and whole-hog reliance on extremely dubious sources in 2003 gave tremendous legitimacy to the Bush administration lies about Iraq possessing weapons of mass destruction—from her beat, but she was not censured formally. Miller herself was unapologetic about her approach to journalism. "My job isn't to assess the government's information and be an independent intelligence analyst myself," she is quoted by Mermin as saying. "My job is to tell readers of the *New York Times* what the government thought about Iraq's arsenal." There, in two stunning sentences, Miller presents the formula for government propaganda, for the news values of authoritarian regimes everywhere including Saddam Hussein's Iraq, and, ultimately, for today's anti-journalism.

As fate would have it, Miller was at her propagandizing peak precisely as the *Times*'s Jayson Blair was run out of the profession in a firestorm of publicity for fabricating stories on mostly low-level matters that cost no human lives. Such a destiny did not await Miller. By 2005, she had been removed from her quasi quarantine, and was given the plum assignment of covering the UN's alleged mismanagement of the Iraqi Oil for Food program. Again, as Russ Baker wrote in *The Nation,* Miller returned to her ways of relying uncritically upon highly partisan Bush administration sources to produce ideologically laden stories. Miller's virtue, according to a *Times* colleague: "[T]hrough her work, people in positions of power speak on the pages of the *New York Times."*

The way the professional code of journalism adapted to the cov-

erage of the occupation of Iraq was not to tell the truth and let the chips fall where they may. As one Baghdad correspondent for a large U.S. newspaper told Michael Massing in October 2004, "the situation in Iraq was a catastrophe," a view shared "almost unanimously" by his colleagues. A widely circulated e-mail in September of 2004 by Farnaz Fassihi, a Baghdad correspondent for the *Wall Street Journal,* was a devastating critique of the U.S. war. "A foreign-policy failure that will haunt the United States for decades to come," Fassihi wrote. She then concluded, "The genie of terrorism, chaos and mayhem has been unleashed onto this country as a result of American mistakes and it can't be put back into the bottle." Massing notes that other U.S. correspondents in Baghdad were startled at the attention Fassihi's e-mail received. "Everyone was marveling and asking what we were doing wrong if that information came as a surprise to the American public," one of them told Massing.

Such a candid view of conditions in Iraq was regarded as partisan, unprofessional, and not objective—regardless of whether or not it was true—because it was a thorough repudiation of the Bush administration position. It was not *balanced,* with balance being defined not by the evidence but by accommodation to powerful interests. This point cannot be overemphasized: The balance that editors employed had nothing to do with the evidence, and everything to do with keeping the Bush administration and the political right off their backs. "Every story from Iraq is by definition an assessment as to whether things are going well or badly," a U.S. newspaper correspondent in Baghdad told Massing. "Editors are hypersensitive about not wanting to appear to be coming down on one side or the other." (There is little evidence that appearing too pro-administration on the war caused many editors to shudder in fear.) Once Fassihi's e-mail was spread across the Internet, the *Wall Street Journal* received pressure to remove her from the beat because she could no longer be regarded as "objective." Fassihi was immediately sent on a vacation until after the November U.S. election, though the *Journal* stated that her break had nothing to do with her e-mail.

Edward Wasserman reflected upon this conundrum in the *Miami Herald.* "I can only imagine the current mind-set of supervising editors: If we give prominence to this story of carnage in Iraq, will we be accused of anti-administration bias? And—here it gets interesting—will we therefore owe our readers an offsetting story, perhaps an inspirational tale of marines teaching young Iraqis how to play softball?" So by following the obsession with balance, the news reports presented a confusing and skewed picture of the reality on the ground in Iraq. And it meant that the logical hard questions that would emerge from tough-minded reporting—like what on earth accounts for this mess?—got lost in the contradictory and incoherent picture provided by balanced reporting. "Balance" did mean that a number of quality reports could get through, especially in the print media. In the months before the November election, there were several first-rate examinations in the mainstream press of the failures of the U.S. occupation. But the TV news coverage was far more pro-war, generally dismissing or ignoring facts that got in the way, with FOX News the exemplar, though far from alone in its patriotic charge.

It did not help matters that John Kerry and leading Democrats did not oppose the war per se, focusing their fire, instead, on, how it was being executed. Kerry was no antiwar candidate, and the war, amazingly enough, was not a defining issue in the 2004 campaign. This meant there was no official antiwar source to embrace what critical reporting there was, draw voter attention to it, and encourage journalists to do more of the same. Not surprisingly, public opinion surveys indicated that in the fall of 2004 a significant percentage of Americans—and most Bush voters—still believed Iraq possessed weapons of mass destruction and that Saddam Hussein was shown to have been a major supporter of al Qaeda, and hence lurked behind the 9/11 attacks. In view of how much media coverage went to these issues, a more thorough repudiation of the press could barely be imagined. (Imagine what we would think of the U.S. media system if in 1944 a survey found a majority of Americans thought China was responsible for the attack on Pearl Harbor?) And the news media routinely accepted the claim from the Bush camp that the president was to be regarded as "strong against terrorism," despite a track record that was open to the opposite characterization.

In sum, the U.S. news media have wanted little part of self-criticism, and no part of locking horns with the Bush administration over an illegal and destabilizing war. It was striking that many U.S. news outlets trumpeted an Associated Press story in March 2005 that a Project for Excellence in Journalism (PEJ) survey established that the number of positive and negative stories in the press about the Iraq war were roughly equivalent. Hence the frequent headline: "Iraq Coverage Wasn't Biased." Case closed in the minds of the media. The coverage was fair and balanced. And the coverage served the public well. Missing in the AP story were the PEJ findings concerning use of sources in war coverage, which were overwhelmingly skewed to pro-war figures.

DEMOCRACY INVARIABLY ASCENDANT

Because the core articles of faith remain inviolable in U.S. journalism and politics, U.S. media coverage of American foreign wars inexorably slides into providing a view compatible with those atop society. Despite the thorough repudiation of every official reason provided by the Bush administration to invade and occupy Iraq, there was almost no effort by journalists to locate more plausible explanations for such a major war. It would not have taken long for an inquiring reporter to find serious experts able to discuss the following factors: the imperial drive encouraged by the existence of a massive military-industrial complex; the geopolitical and economic advantages from having permanent military bases and a client regime/friendly ally in the heart of the Middle East; the domestic political advantages for a president to have the populace whipped into wartime fervor; the security needs of Israel, the close ally of the United States; and, of course, oil. Such explanations can be found in elite journals, in the business press, in intelligence reports, and in academic studies. Such an approach is applied in popular analyses of the motives of any other nation, but such inquiry was and is off-limits in U.S. politics and in U.S. mainstream journalism. To our leading politicians and journalists, the United States is a benevolent nation, always working with the ultimate objective of promoting democracy.

When the United States finally convened an election in Iraq on January 30, it was trumpeted with a massive PR blitz by Washington, and the media obediently responded. The election was regarded as a wondrous democratic moment and viewed without criticism in the news media. Finally, the war was won! And, finally, too, the truth could come out for why the United States had invaded and occupied Iraq: to bring democracy to the entire Middle East and, of course, to liberate the women! This explanation was embraced across the political spectrum, as it tapped into the core presuppositions about the U.S. role in the world. Bill Maher, the political comedian who had his ABC program cancelled following post–9/11 comments seen by the political right as insufficiently jingoistic, and who had been a sharp opponent of Bush and the invasion of Iraq, embraced the new Wilsonian vision. "Maybe we were wrong," Maher told the liberal audience of his HBO program. Since the war was for democracy, and had succeeded, it was now a good war. Sure, it would have been nice if Bush had leveled with us in the first place and told us the war was about installing democracy in Iraq, but that is minor compared to the fact that Bush was right to invade Iraq to install democracy.

When pressed for evidence that democracy was flowering, Maher simply stated, without his usual sense of irony, "Read the papers." Yes, but which newspapers? Should one rely upon those media that had been hoodwinked by the U.S. government about the reasons for war and had served as propagandists for the invasion? Or should one turn to those journalists who had been properly skeptical toward U.S. war claims and who had been proven correct? Logic would suggest the latter group of reporters had a much higher batting average as far as the truth is concerned. Had Maher taken the time to read the dispatches of Naomi Klein, Jonathan Steele, or other reporters on the ground in Iraq who had *not* been taken in by the earlier U.S. justifications for invasion and occupation, he would have seen strong arguments that the notion that this was now a U.S. war for democracy was at best dubious. As Robert Dreyfuss put it three months after the election, as Iraqi politicians struggled to form a government: "The catch-22 is this: To gain legitimacy in the eyes of Iraq's population, and to avoid being seen as puppets, the new government has to distance itself from the U.S. occupation forces. Doing so, however, is impossible, since the newly elected regime wouldn't last a week without the protection of U.S. forces. So they are stuck in a fatal embrace." But that perspective apparently was not in the U.S. papers upon which Maher relied. There, democracy was ascendant.

Or, possibly, what reporters on the ground in Iraq were experiencing was not being conveyed accurately due to the obsession with balance. The reality on the ground was so permanently damning of the U.S. occupation, that in their hunger for balance, U.S. editors bit on any Bush administration propaganda blitz to show improvement. Moreover, the situation was so tense in Iraq that few U.S. journalists had the capacity to get outside of the heavily barricaded Green Zone to generate much of an independent view. Three months after the election and the birth of democracy, Andrew Ackerman reported in *Editor & Publisher* that U.S. war reporters in Iraq still found the nation "uncommonly dangerous and difficult." For safety reasons few reporters ever ventured beyond a very narrow sliver of the nation and admittedly had little direct idea of what was happening in the country. The conditions made it almost impossible to do journalism; as a *Dallas Morning News* photographer put it, "spending more than twenty minutes at a news scene can be deadly." "It's like a military operation every time we go to a press conference in the Green Zone, even just a regular press conference," said a correspondent for the *Washington Post.* But even from their hotel rooms, U.S. correspondents understood the election might not have been the turning point in a war of liberation. Hannah Allam, the Baghdad bureau chief for Knight Ridder questioned the idea that democratic Iraq would soon be free of its liberators. "But when you see these bases, these are not makeshift tent cities," she wrote of the U.S. occupation force. "They poured in millions and millions of dollars into these facilities. It's clear that they're there to stay."

As the United States celebrated the triumph of freedom and democracy, elementary questions went unasked. On what grounds should the U.S. claim to be concerned with democracy be taken seriously? (At the same time George W. Bush was leading his democratic crusade in Iraq, the murderous dictator of Uzbekistan, Islam Karimov, who could certainly give Saddam Hussein a run for his money in the human rights violations department, was called "very much George W. Bush's man in Central Asia," by the former British ambassador to Uzbekistan.) Is the United States a philanthropy that has no military or economic designs? Why did U.S. occupation authorities in Iraq work so hard to delay elections? If the U.S. favors democratic rule, why ignore the fact that most Iraqis voted for parties calling for a near-term or immediate end to the U.S. occupation? Is it legitimate to invade a nation to install democracy? If it is legitimate, who makes the decision about which country to invade and who does the invading? If the United States can do it to Iraq, can India do it to Pakistan? Can Russia invade Uzbekistan? Can Venezuela invade Colombia? Can Canada look at inequities in our society (toward women and ethnic minorities) or at irregularities in our voting procedures and determine that it needs to invade the United States to establish a bona fide democracy?

Even if we all agree that it is all right to invade a country to install democracy and that the United States is the legitimate force to do so, is Iraq the first nation on the list that should be invaded? Why not Pakistan? Or Saudi Arabia? Or Kuwait? Who is next? Is every non-democracy in need of an invasion or just some? Which ones? These are the questions that must be answered to justify a democratic invasion. Otherwise this is just the law of the jungle, with all talk about democracy, which is predicated upon the rule of law, so much bunkum, and should be acknowledged as such. In our media system, these questions almost never get asked; the subject never gets sustained attention.

JOURNALISM AS FARCE

Indeed, even when all the questions are answered—and evidence of official wrongdoing is handed to reporters on a silver platter—U.S. media cannot be counted on to "do" the story.

The controversy surrounding the documents that came to be known as the "Downing Street memo" revealed the depth to which journalistic standards at major-media outlets in the U.S. have sunk. The secret memorandums, which were first revealed by an investigative reporter for the *Times* of London, detailed behind-closed-doors discussions involving British intelligence aides and members of Prime Minister Tony Blair's inner circle from the period in 2002 when the Bush White House was pressuring Britain to back the president's plan to invade Iraq. Blair's lieutenants were skeptical about the likelihood that they could convince the British people of the need to go to war based on the flimsy arguments put forward so far. But Sir Richard Dearlove, the chief of the country's MI6 intelligence unit, assured them that the Bush administration was busy "fixing the intelligence and facts" in order to foster the fantasy that action was called for.

Without a doubt, this was a classic "smoking gun" revelation, and the European media treated it as such when the story came to light in the spring of 2005. What more could journalists ask for than evidence that the big boss of British intelligence had secretly acknowledged that the president and his aides had faked the case for what it was generally agreed had turned out to be a disastrous military adventure?

Yet, while British reporters had a field day with the story, major media outlets in the U.S. ignored it for more than a month and then—under intense pressure from Americans who had learned about the memo from the Internet—finally responded by dismissing it as "old news" because, after all, everyone knew that George Bush had decided to go to war long before he admitted as much to the American people.

The refusal to treat the Downing Street memo story seriously was all the more staggering in light of what U.S. media outlets chose to cover in May and June of 2005. Arianna Huffington's website HuffBlog reported in late June on a study of the big stories of those months. Between May 1 and June 20, ABC News did 121 segments on the Michael Jackson trial, 42 on Natalee Holloway, an Alabama teenager who went missing in Aruba, and *zero* on the story of the White House falsifying the "case" for war. CBS news did 235 segments on Jackson, 70 on Holloway, and *zero* on the Downing Street memo. NBC did 109 segments on Jackson, 62 on Holloway, and six on Downing Street.

In a condemnation of what he referred to as "a press coverup" by "the Beltway herd," writer Joe Conason demolished the lame excuses of U.S. media managers and journalists for failing to cover the memo story.

"Only a very special brand of arrogance would permit any employee of the *New York Times,* which brought us the mythmaking of Judith Miller, to insist that new documentary evidence of 'intelligence fixing' about Saddam's arsenal is no longer news," wrote Conason.

> The same goes for the *Washington Post,* which featured phony administration claims about Iraq's weapons on Page 1 while burying the skeptical stories that proved correct. If you listen to those mooing most loudly, such as the editorial page editors of the *Post,* the Downing Street memo still isn't news because it doesn't "prove" anything. (Only the *Post* would refer to Sir Richard Dearlove, the chief of Britain's MI6 intelligence service who reported the fixing of intelligence to fit Bush's war plans, as merely "a British official.") Certainly it proves much about the candid views held by the most knowledgeable figures in the British government. Evidently the *Post*'s editorialists would rather not learn what else the memo might prove if its clues were investigated.) How foolish and how sad that all these distinguished journalists prefer to transform this scandal into a debate about their own underachieving performance, rather than redeem mainstream journalism by advancing an important story that they should have pursued from the beginning. This is a moment when the mainstream press could again demonstrate to a skeptical

public why we need journalists. Instead they are proving once more that their first priority is to cover their own behinds.

Writing a month and a half after the story broke, Conason explained:

Deciding what constitutes news is a subjective exercise, of course, with all the uncertainty that implies. Yet there are several obvious guidelines to keep in mind while listening to the excuses proffered in the *New York Times* and the *Washington Post* by reporters who must know better. A classified document recording deliberations by the highest officials of our most important ally over the decision to wage war is always news. A document that shows those officials believed the justification for war was "thin" and that the intelligence was being "fixed" is always news. A document that indicates the president was misleading the world about his determination to wage war only as a last resort is always news. And when such a document is leaked, whatever editors, reporters and producers may think "everyone" already knows or believes about its contents emphatically does not affect whether that piece of paper is news. The journalists' job is to determine whether it is authentic and then to probe into its circumstances and meaning. There are many questions still to be answered about the Downing Street memo, but the nation's most prominent journalists still aren't asking them.

In an effort to draw attention to the information contained in the British documents, U.S. Representative John Conyers, D-Michigan, the ranking Democrat on the House Judiciary Committee, organized a June, 2005, hearing on Capitol Hill. Instead of biting on a story that was literally being handed to them, however, some of the top reporters in the country literally ridiculed Conyers for trying to get to the bottom of a scandal that former White House counsel John Dean has correctly identified as "worse than Watergate."

Washington Post writer Dana Milbank penned a snarly little piece that, like similar articles in the *New York Times* and other "newspapers of record," displayed all the concern for accuracy, hunger for truth, and skepticism regarding Bush administration misdeeds that one might expect to find in a White House press release.

To his credit, Conyers hit back.

In a letter addressed to the *Post*'s national editor, the newspaper's ombudsman, and Milbank, the veteran House member was blunt. It deserves to be reprinted in its entirety.

"Dear Sirs," Conyers began,

I write to express my profound disappointment with Dana Milbank's June 17 report, "Democrats Play House to Rally Against the War," which purports to describe a Democratic hearing I chaired in the Capitol yesterday. In sum, the piece cherry-picks some facts, manufactures others out of whole cloth, and does a disservice to some 30 members of Congress who persevered under difficult circumstances, not of our own making, to examine a very serious subject: whether the American people were deliberately misled in the lead up to war. The fact that this was the *Post*'s only coverage of this event makes the journalistic shortcomings in this piece even more egregious.

In an inaccurate piece of reporting that typifies the article, Milbank implies that one of the obstacles the members in the meeting have is that "only one" member has mentioned the Downing Street Minutes on the floor of either the House or Senate. This is not only incorrect but misleading. In fact, just yesterday, the Senate Democratic Leader, Harry Reid, mentioned it on the Senate floor. Senator Boxer talked at some length about it at the recent confirmation hearing for the Ambassador to Iraq. The House Democratic Leader,

Nancy Pelosi, recently signed on to my letter, along with 121 other Democrats asking for answers about the memo. This information is not difficult to find either. For example, the Reid speech was the subject of an AP wire service report posted on the *Washington Post* website with the headline "Democrats Cite Downing Street Memo in Bolton Fight." Other similar mistakes, mischaracterizations and cheap shots are littered throughout the article.

The article begins with an especially mean and nasty tone, claiming that House Democrats "pretended" a small conference room was the Judiciary Committee hearing room and deriding the decor of the room. Milbank fails to share with his readers one essential fact: the reason the hearing was held in that room, an important piece of context. Despite the fact that a number of other suitable rooms were available in the Capitol and House office buildings, Republicans declined my request for each and every one of them. Milbank could have written about the perseverance of many of my colleagues in the face of such adverse circumstances, but declined to do so. Milbank also ignores the critical fact picked up by the AP, CNN and other newsletters that at the very moment the hearing was scheduled to begin, the Republican Leadership scheduled an almost unprecedented number of 11 consecutive floor votes, making it next to impossible for most Members to participate in the first hour and one half of the hearing.

In what can only be described as a deliberate effort to discredit the entire hearing, Milbank quotes one of the witnesses as making an anti-Semitic assertion and further describes anti-Semitic literature that was being handed out in the overflow room for the event. First, let me be clear: I consider myself to be a friend and supporter of Israel and there were a number of other staunchly pro-Israel members who were in attendance at the hearing. I do not agree with, sup-

port, or condone any comments asserting Israeli control over
U.S. policy, and I find any allegation that Israel is trying to
dominate the world or had anything to do with the September 11 tragedy disgusting and offensive.

That said, to give such emphasis to 100 seconds of a 3 hour and five minute hearing that included the powerful and sad testimony (hardly mentioned by Milbank) of a woman who lost her son in the Iraq war and now feels lied to as a result of the Downing Street Minutes, is incredibly misleading. Many, many different pamphlets were being passed out at the overflow room, including pamphlets about getting out of the Iraq war and anti-Central American Free Trade Agreement, and it is puzzling why Milbank saw fit to only mention the one he did.

In a typically derisive and uninformed passage, Milbank makes much of other lawmakers calling me "Mr. Chairman" and says I liked it so much that I used "chairmanly phrases." Milbank may not know that I was the Chairman of the House Government Operations Committee from 1988 to 1994. By protocol and tradition in the House, once you have been a Chairman you are always referred to as such. Thus, there was nothing unusual about my being referred to as Mr. Chairman.

To administer his coup-de-grace, Milbank literally makes up another cheap shot that I "was having so much fun that [I] ignored aides' entreaties to end the session." This did not occur. None of my aides offered entreaties to end the session and I have no idea where Milbank gets that information. The hearing certainly ran longer than expected, but that was because so many Members of Congress persevered under very difficult circumstances to attend, and I thought—given that—the least I could do was allow them to say their piece. That is called courtesy, not "fun."

By the way, the "Downing Street Memo" is actually the

minutes of a British cabinet meeting. In the meeting, British officials—having just met with their American counterparts—describe their discussions with such counterparts. I mention this because that basic piece of context, a simple description of the memo, is found nowhere in Milbank's article.

The fact that I and my fellow Democrats had to stuff a hearing into a room the size of a large closet to hold a hearing on an important issue shouldn't make us the object of ridicule. In my opinion, the ridicule should be placed in two places: first, at the feet of Republicans who are so afraid to discuss ideas and facts that they try to sabotage our efforts to do so; and second, on Dana Milbank and the *Washington Post,* who do not feel the need to give serious coverage on a serious hearing about a serious matter—whether more than 1,700 Americans have died because of a deliberate lie. Milbank may disagree, but the *Post* certainly owed its readers some coverage of that viewpoint.

Sincerely, John Conyers, Jr.

The years of the Bush presidency will be remembered as a time when American media, for the most part, practiced stenography to power—and when once-great newspapers became little more than what the reformers of another time referred to as "the kept press."

The Conyers letter, like the thousands of communications from grassroots activists to media outlets across this country pressing for serious coverage of the "Downing Street Memo" and the broader debate about the Bush administration's doctoring of intelligence prior to the launch of the Iraq war, is an essential response to our contemporary media crisis. That it had to be written provides evidence not of the decline of American journalism, but of its complete collapse as a source of needed information for citizens who would choose to be their own governors.

THE DEATH OF CITIZEN CONTROL OF THE MILITARY

One can be a proponent of an aggressive U.S. military role in the world and also a democrat. But to be both requires a commitment to effective civilian control over the war-making power of the republic, and that requires a viable press system. The notion that a self-appointed and privileged elite can "handle the truth" about why the United States invades other nations or overthrows their governments, but the great unwashed mass needs to be bathed in a cocktail of propaganda and lies, decontextualized half-truths, and jingoism to get their support is repugnant. Yet our media system and our official political culture have failed to protect democratic control over the war-making process. Their performance goes directly against the Madisonian vision, the spirit of our Constitution, and it will require fundamental changes in our political culture and our media system to rectify.

The dreadful media coverage of the U.S. invasion of Iraq did produce one significant unintended consequence: It fueled the emerging media reform movement that we discuss in chapter 6. During the spring of 2003, as millions of Americans organized to protest the coming invasion, many of them were outraged by the rabidly pro-war nature of the media coverage. At the time, Russ Baker characterized the FOX News Channel "as a kind of *Gong Show* of propaganda," and he noted that "FOX is actually more gung-ho in its support of the war than U.S. government entities like Radio Free Europe/Radio Liberty." Jim Rutenberg in the *New York Times* wrote about the "FOX Effect," whereby the other cable news channels tried to match FOX's pro-war enthusiasm.

Phil Donahue's MSNBC program was the exception, and it was under strict guidelines to have a majority of its guests be pro-administration, since Donahue was a liberal. No other cable news show was under similar guidelines; no conservative hosts were required to have a majority of their guests for every program be anti-administration. Donahue's program was cancelled by MSNBC in February 2003 after an internal memo stated that he represented "a difficult public face for NBC in a time of war." The memo expressed alarm that Donahue's show would become "a home for the liberal antiwar agenda at the same time that our competitors are waving the flag at every opportunity." As Donahue was being terminated, MSNBC was adding conservative shows hosted by pro-war former congressman Joe Scarborough, and by talk radio host Michael Savage, who told his MSNBC audience that those opposing the war "are absolutely committing sedition, or treason."

People began to understand in a profound manner the importance of the media front to the exercise of war.

At the exact moment that the United States invaded Iraq, the FCC was in the midst of its review of media ownership rules. When groups like MoveOn.org informed their million plus members that the same media firms—Rupert Murdoch's News Corporation, Clear Channel, General Electric, Tribune Company, Sinclair Broadcast Group—that were shilling for the war were now looking to the Bush administration to relax media ownership rules so they could gobble up what remained of the U.S. media system, it was like setting a match to a canister of gasoline. The sleaziness and corruption of the Bush-media relationship, of the media system itself, was palpable. Big media firms push Bush's war, and Bush allows them to establish more monopolistic power, and decimate local ownership. FCC Chairman Michael Powell poured more gasoline on the flames when he declared that the "thrilling" TV coverage of the war proved there was nothing to be concerned about with regard to media consolidation. MoveOn leaders stated they got the most enthusiastic response ever from their membership when they broached the idea of opposing media concentration. Other antiwar groups, such as CODEPINK: Women for Peace, had a similar response. Not long after the war began, a CODEPINK Action Alert read, "Think there has been 'fair and balanced' media coverage on the invasion of Iraq? No? Well it's going to get worse unless we stop the consolidation." A movement was being born.

CHAPTER 4

THE POLICING OF THE PRIMARIES

"The good news for us is that Dean is not the nominee."

—Karl Rove, February 2004

Karl Rove knew that he, or, to be precise, the hapless Texan whose presidential campaign he was managing, could beat John Kerry.

But Rove did not necessarily believe George W. Bush could beat *any* Democrat.

So, considering the fact that Rove was the media-crowned master of the electoral universe in 2004, it would seem that the most interesting political question of the year was not "How did Rove win it?" but rather "Who did Rove fear?" It's not just that enquiring minds might want to know. Getting the story of how Rove got the opponent he wanted, as opposed to the opponent he feared, was essential to answering the question of how the election finished the way it did.

Yet, for the most part, political reporters failed to ask the questions that mattered during the 2004 campaign season; indeed, they actually fell for the fantasy that Rove feared Kerry most. So most Americans never knew the identity of the Democrat whose candidacy caused the White House political czar sleepless nights.

Only the few intrepid citizens who read to the very end of Bob Woodward's inside-with-the-insiders tale of how the Bush administration led the United States into the Iraq imbroglio, *Plan of Attack*—an exercise in long-distance reading that appears to have been too demanding for the vast majority of political journalists—knew that Rove had a least-favorite Democrat.

In the epilogue of his book, Woodward describes how the man they call "Bush's brain" saw the presidential race in February 2004.

Noting that Rove believed the war in Iraq was turning into "a potential negative" for the Bush-Cheney reelection campaign, Woodward wrote, "Previously, Rove had claimed he was salivating at the prospect that the Democrats would nominate former Vermont Governor Howard Dean in the 2004 presidential race. But Dean had imploded and Senator John Kerry, the Massachusetts Democrat, had won twelve of the first fourteen Democratic primary contests and it looked like he was headed for the nomination."

What did Rove have to say about this development? " 'The good news for us is that Dean is not the nominee,' Rove now argued to an associate in his second-floor West Wing office. Dean's unconditional opposition to the Iraq War could have been potent in a face-off with Bush. One of Dean's strengths was he could say, 'I'm not part of that crowd down there.' But Kerry was very much a part of the Washington crowd and he had voted in favor of the resolution for war. Rove got out his two-inch-thick loose-leaf binder titled 'Bring It On.' It consisted of research into Kerry's 19-year record in the Senate. Most relevant were pages 9–20 of the section on Iraq."

Woodward explained that, "Rove believed they had Kerry pretty cold on voting to give the president a green light for war and then backing off when he didn't like the aftermath or saw a political opportunity. Whatever the case, Rove sounded as if he believed they could inoculate the president on the Iraq War in a campaign with Kerry."

"Rove," Woodward observed, "was gleeful."

And rightly so.

But, since Karl Rove isn't supposed to be in charge of picking George W. Bush's opponents, how was it that he got exactly what he wanted? How was it that John Kerry, the Hamlet of American politics, ended up carrying the Democratic banner against Bush, as opposed to the Democrat that Rove and other Republicans secretly feared?

There is little evidence to suggest that Rove himself meddled in the Democratic primaries in the way that Richard Nixon's henchmen waded into the opposition party's nominating process in 1972. He didn't have to break any laws. All Rove did was dish out self-serving spin to the lapdogs of the White House press corps. And there can be no doubt that this played some role in fostering what we now know was a false impression that Republican insiders relished a race against a fiery critic of the president's failed foreign policies. Rove's spin wasn't all that different from what Democratic powerbrokers—who saw Dean as an interloper from the la-la land of Vermont—were peddling. And it came with the same intent.

What Rove and other insiders—from both sides of the partisan aisle—relied upon was the absolute certainty that DC-based celebrity journalists and pundits would be just as horrified as they were at the prospect that a renegade contender might filch the Democratic nomination. The political elites of Washington know that big media plays a well-marked role in defining the choices from which America's two major parties select their nominees for president. The United States has an informal two-party system—it exists without Constitutional mandate or legal parameters at the federal level—that is maintained in large part by the determination of major media outlets to treat Democrats and Republicans as the only political players who matter. Third parties, as Ralph Nader discovered in 2000 when he mounted a serious national campaign but was not allowed to set foot on the stages of the fall debates, are dismissed as spoilers at best, nuisances and cranks in general, and downright un-American at worst. The news media police the boundaries of the political system, and they do so very effectively.

But even within the two existing parties it is not a level playing field. Where once political bosses decided which candidates would be considered viable, now a pack of political journalists—most of whom live in Washington and spend non-election years covering the White House and Congress—do the vetting. And, as with the coverage of policy debates in the nation's capitol, the coverage of the campaigns for the respective presidential nominations of the two major parties are carefully choreographed to reflect the biases of the Washington elites. Those candidates who have the most money, and who are most closely connected to power, tend to receive not only more attention but also more favorable coverage than dissidents mounting populist challenges. The established candidates flood the corporate media coffers with huge checks to purchase mostly asinine TV ads; this establishes their credibility as serious candidates in the minds of the media. Indeed, TV advertising often comes to set the agenda for what journalists write about and pundits bloviate about. The degree of difficulty for a grassroots candidate to win a national election in the United States would be high under the best of circumstances; with the wholesale resistance of the news media the chances have become astronomically difficult.

As illustration of how the process works, in this chapter we examine the latest manifestation of the phenomenon: The rise and fall of the Howard Dean campaign of 2003–04. What is striking here is not simply the policing of dissidents by political pack journalism. Dean may well have survived that; after all, he was far from a radical. To the contrary, what was striking in 2004 was simply the utter decline of political journalism to a point where it could be so easily manipulated to derail a campaign that inspired such enthusiasm at the party's grass roots.

ESCORTING THE DEVIANTS TO THE MARGINS

The storyline developed by the political and media punditocracy—once separate entities that are now virtually indistinguishable—has it that Howard Dean did himself in. To be sure, the Vermont governor was a flawed champion who had a hard time making the transit from also-ran to frontrunner, and who was unable to right the course of his campaign when it derailed in the Iowa caucuses of January 2004. But, as the year's fall campaign would illustrate, Kerry was not without his own flaws. And the truth of the story about how Kerry became the nominee, rather than Dean, had a good deal more to do with the desires of political insiders in Washington, and the media that churns out their spin under the "news and analysis" label than it did with the candidates or the electorate. It is not at all unreasonable to suggest that the media played a more definitional role in determining the identity of the Democratic nominee against George W. Bush than did the grassroots Democrats who so passionately wanted to defeat the president. Nor is it too much to say that, because the media played the role it did, Karl Rove got the election he wanted rather than the one he feared.

Rick Salutin, the Canadian playwright and media critic who observes the drama of American politics with a detached but keen eye, explained from the safe distance of Toronto that, "The media are the ushers and the security guards of politics. They maintain decorum. Salutin noted with far more accuracy than most American commentators that when Dean mounted the sort of campaign that disturbed the decorum of the contest by saying the sort of things that excited grassroots Democrats, scared Karl Rove, and could have given America the sort of campaign that befits a great democracy, a media that is "professionally conditioned to spot incoming threats" identified the former Vermont governor as an electoral "deviant" and escorted him "to the political margins."

The notion that the media police the political landscape in America is not a new one.

More than a century ago, the populists and progressives who sought to wrestle control of the country from the oligarchs of another age recognized that they could not count on newspapers, the dominant media of their day, to cover political insurgency with the impartiality, let alone the sympathy, that it merited. If anything, the complaints voiced by contemporary media critics are tepid compared with those of the author Theodore Dreiser, who observed that, "The American press, with a very few exceptions, is a kept press. Kept by the big corporations the way a whore is kept by a rich man." The kept press of Dreiser's day may have been on a short leash, but it was always given enough slack to rip apart presidential contenders who upset the decorum of America's parlor politics, as supporters of William Jennings Bryan, Eugene Victor Debs, Robert M. La Follette, and other insurgent candidates who fell afoul of the owners of the nation's largest daily newspapers learned in the bitter campaigns of 1896, 1900, 1908, 1912, 1920, and 1924.

But a century ago media ownership was far more diversified than it is today, and it was dramatically easier for challenging ideas to reach a mass audience via opposition publications. In the early years of the twentieth century, many major cities had at least a half dozen English-language daily newspapers and at least that many foreign-language publications—New York alone had six Yiddish-language dailies, most of them left-leaning. The number of daily newspapers in the U.S. actually peaked in 1910 at two thousand six hundred, and among their number were dozens that advocated for radical reform. By 1912, Socialists were publishing more than three hundred daily, weekly, and monthly publications, including Julius A. Wayland's *Appeal to Reason,* which reached a circulation of seven hundred sixty thousand in 1913 and was the first place of publication for Upton Sinclair's novel *The Jungle.* The great muckraking newspapers and magazines of the day found their way into more than twenty million American households and inspired movements for workplace safety, food quality, and clean government, and were more radical than anything seen in recent decades in the U.S. Indeed, Indiana senator Albert Beveridge credited the "people's literature" of the muckrakers with inspiring a wave of reform that was "almost a mental and moral revolution."

The word "almost" was well chosen, as government repression during and after World War I, as well as pressure from advertisers who did not take kindly to exposés of corporate misdeeds, soon began to kill off dissident and questioning publications. As community after community witnessed the death of newspaper competition, the modern model of a one-size-fits-all media that sets the parameters for debate and punishes those candidates who dare to step beyond the lines of limitation, even when they do so in interesting and thought-provoking ways that ought to excite red-blooded journalists, took shape. Where the policing of the process was once idiosyncratic— "Mr. Hearst doesn't like this guy, so we're going to smear him," or even "Wall Street doesn't like this guy . . ."—it has now become systemic. Afraid to be accused by the Right or the Left of bias, media managers and their employees simply head for the safe ground of conventional wisdom and insider preference.

The whole process has been dumbed down, as candidates are penalized for being too serious, too passionate, or, simply, too interesting. Election campaigns are referred to as "cycles" or "seasons" and build up to the "Super Bowl" of the quadrennial presidential vote. Polls are given far more credence than evidence of grassroots organization; candidates who talk too much about the issues are dismissed as being "off message"; the personal stories and personality quirks of the various contenders and even members of their extended families are given so much attention that following a campaign feels a bit like watching the celebrity trial of a Michael Jackson or an O. J. Simpson. No wonder citizens—almost half of whom do not bother to vote— feel as if they are being invited to step to the sidelines to watch a horse race. Media for Democracy 2004, a non-partisan citizens' initiative developed to monitor mainstream news coverage of the 2004 election and advocate fair, democratic, and issue-oriented standards of reporting, reviewed coverage of the campaign from the critical weeks leading up to the Iowa caucuses and the New Hampshire primary in January 2004. What they found was that, during this most critical month of campaigning for the presidential nomination of one of the nation's two major parties, less than 5 percent of the network TV broadcasts regarding the race dealt with candidates' positions on policy issues, such as health care, education, the war in Iraq, the economy, or employment. According to Media for Democracy, "Candidates are increasingly not being identified according to their stances on the issues. As a result, too much of the coverage emphasizes the process itself over substance and issues."

The warped primary campaign of 2004 represented the latest loss of ground on a slippery slope that began to give way a century ago. With the passage of each decade of the twentieth century, the discourse in the United States has narrowed, so that today it is virtually unimaginable that a proponent of radical reform could get the hearing that even Robert M. La Follette did in 1924 when he won almost five million votes, carried Wisconsin, ran second in eleven Western states, and swept working-class Jewish and Italian wards of New York and other major cities, providing the rough outline for the rural-urban populist coalition that eight years later would provide Franklin Roosevelt and the New Deal Democrats with their base of support.

Howard Dean was no La Follette, and it is probably worth noting here that neither of us supported his candidacy. In the early stages of the campaign, we saw him as a rather dull centrist who was unlikely to be much of a change agent. Even in the end, he was less a radical than a moderate former governor who embraced a few mainstream liberal and progressive ideas in 2003, recognized the political potential of the Internet, and finished the pre-campaign of 2003 as the clear front-runner for the Democratic presidential nomination of 2004.

What interested us about Dean was the way in which the rise and fall of his candidacy illustrates the extent to which the media as it is currently configured serves both as a political gatekeeper and, when a renegade presidential candidate jumps the fence, as a sharpshooter trained to finish off the offending contender before the vast majority of Americans have a chance to vote for something other than the lesser of two evils. In other words, it is the media, not the candidates, and certainly not the voters, that end up defending the status quo. We understand, of course, that the media are not monolithic. FOX's Bill O'Reilly's approach is a whole lot different from that of Democracy Now's Amy Goodman. But it should not come as news to anyone that, for the most part, reporters for major media outlets tend to operate as a pack when covering presidential campaigns. And when the pack turns on a candidate, he or she will soon begin to feel like the foxes must have before hunts were outlawed.

DECIDING WHICH CANDIDATES ARE CREDIBLE

Dean was both a beneficiary and a victim of the media's policing of the 2004 presidential election campaign. Early on, the patrician politician with the same pedigree of private-school preparation and Yale degrees as Kerry and Bush was a favorite of elite political reporters who enjoy the sport of pumping up the prospects of a brainy candidate who is going nowhere—Bruce Babbitt in 1988, Paul Tsongas in 1992, Bill Bradley in 2000—in order to create the impression that the process is fluid enough and interesting enough to justify their expensive travel budgets to the bean counters who now make most of the decisions about the extent to which campaigns are covered. In the spring and summer of 2003, Dean was the flavor of the month, and then of the next month, and then of the month after that. But a funny thing happened on the way to the political scrapheap: Dean's campaign took off. He started topping the polls, leading in fund raising, and attracting the endorsements of prominent Democrats such as former Vice President Al Gore, Illinois U.S. Representative Jesse Jackson Jr., and Iowa Senator Tom Harkin.

When the media policeman was his friend, Dean could do no wrong. Indeed, lesser-known but certainly credible liberal and progressive contenders were elbowed aside by reporters seeking to promote a "clear"—translation: easy to cover—contest between Dean and the inside-the-beltway favorites who, by virtue of having appeared frequently enough on *Face the Nation* and *Meet the Press,* were designated even before the race began as front-runners: Kerry, Connecticut Senator Joe Lieberman, North Carolina Senator John Edwards, and Missouri Representative Dick Gephardt. Added to the list of serious candidates was retired General Wesley Clark, whose claim to credibility as a national political contender appears to have had a lot to do with his stint as a military-affairs commentator for CNN.

Notably absent from the list of credible contenders were the three candidates whose progressive stances on the issues most clearly mirrored those expressed by grassroots Democrats in surveys: the two African-American contenders for the nomination, the Reverend Al Sharpton and former Illinois Senator Carole Moseley Braun, and the co-chair of the Congressional Progressive Caucus, Ohio Representative Dennis Kucinich. All three of the "dismissed" candidates knew the issues, all three had staked out stances that were bolder and more detailed than those of the supposed front-runners, and all three were dramatically more articulate than Kerry or several of the other media favorites, as the debates between the Democratic candidates would repeatedly illustrate. Sharpton had never held public office and came to the race with a record of stirring controversy in his native New York, while Moseley Braun had been bumped from her Senate seat in 1998 following a single term in which she had been dogged by ethics complaints. But Kucinich, a scrappy former mayor of Cleveland who had beaten Republican incumbents to win state and federal positions and had been repeatedly reelected to a U.S. House seat representing a swing district that included the politically competitive suburbs of his hometown, had emerged as a champion of progressive positions in Congress, earning a good deal of attention, mainly via the Internet, for a pointed antiwar speech he delivered to a major Americans for Democratic Action event in Southern California.

The only candidate with a proven track record of winning tough elections in districts dominated by the sort of white working-class voters that both parties had been competing for since the 1980s when many of the voters abandoned their Democratic roots to back Republican Ronald Reagan, Kucinich should have attracted a reasonable amount of attention from political journalists who had written millions of words and taped thousands of segments on what Democrats and Republicans would be doing in 2004 to woo voters who had come to be known as "Reagan Democrats."

PUNISHING SERIOUSNESS

Unfortunately for Kucinich, he could not get a break from big media.

The Progressive Caucus co-chair ran a vigorous, intellectually adventurous, policy-based campaign for the nomination. He leaped on issues before the other candidates—including Dean—recognized them. He brought broader perspectives to the debates and he built a national network of supporters that would eventually develop into one of the more interesting Democratic activist groups to survive the 2004 campaign, Progressive Democrats of America. Yet, the political punditocracy steadfastly refused to treat his candidacy with even a measure of the seriousness that was accorded the other members of the House and Senate who were seeking the party's nod.

One argument was that Kucinich, who never made much of a dent in the national polls, simply got the coverage he deserved. While it is true that Kucinich always fell short of front-runner status, his supporters griped that he was at least as viable a candidate as Connecticut Senator Joe Lieberman, a centrist Democrat who echoed Bush administration stances on the war in Iraq and global trade. But, where Lieberman was a regular on the television talk shows, Kucinich was rarely invited. The griping of Kucinich supporters about media bias against his candidacy had a ring of legitimacy to the ears of John Green, director of the University of Akron's Ray C. Bliss Institute.

"It's a legitimate complaint," Green, a veteran observer of the media's impact on political races, told the *Akron Beacon Journal* during the early stages of the campaign.

"The media, particularly television, cover elections like horse races," Green explained, noting that in the 2004 horse race, television reporters tended to dismiss Kucinich as the "fringe candidate" or the "long-shot candidate" from the start, creating a catch-22 from which the candidate could not free himself.

The absurdity, and the irresponsibility, of most media's approach to Kucinich's candidacy was particularly evident in the fall of 2003, as the campaign for the Democratic nomination hit its stride.

Take the case of the debate about the reliability of voting systems—an issue that would achieve a reasonably high profile a year
later, as millions of Americans expressed doubts about whether results
from Ohio, the state that tipped the presidential race to Bush, were
accurate.

Typically, Kucinich was ahead of the curve on an important issue.
In November 2003, he seized on concerns about the reliability of
electronic voting machines produced by Diebold, Inc., one of the
nation's largest voting equipment manufacturers. Those concerns
were stirred by the revelation that Diebold employees had expressed
concerns in e-mails about the security of machines produced by the
company.

Diebold sought to shut down any debate about its machines by
threatening legal actions against operators of websites that were publishing or linking to corporate documents that detailed flaws in
Diebold equipment and irregularities in the certifying of the
company's systems for counting and tabulating votes.

When he learned of the legal threats, Kucinich took on the politically potent corporation. The Ohio congressman asked House Judiciary Committee chairman Jim Sensenbrenner (R-Wisconsin), and
the ranking Democrat on that committee, Representative John
Conyers of Michigan, to investigate whether the company's actions
were potential abuses of the Digital Millennium Copyright Act. He
also posted the controversial documents on his congressional website.

Diebold quickly backed down. And Kucinich used the development to declare, "In a democracy where half the people don't vote
and where the last presidential election was decided by the Supreme
Court, we cannot tolerate flawed voting equipment or intimidation
of those who point out the flaws. Diebold backing down from its intimidation campaign is a positive step. An open and honest examination of the flaws in electronic voting will lead us to only one possible
conclusion: electronic voting machines are dangerous to democracy
because there is no way of ensuring their accuracy. We have to have a

voter-verified paper trail for every election so that any errors and irregularities caused by the voting machines can be recovered."

All in all, that made for a meaty story—or, at least, what should
have been a meaty story. A presidential candidate took on a major
corporation and won a fight over an issue that was, by any reasonable
measures, fundamental to the functioning of American democracy.

So were there newspaper headlines about Kucinich's fight with
Diebold? No. Television news reports? No. Lengthy discussions on
commercial talk radio? No.

Indeed, the story on Kucinich that got extensive coverage in the
late fall of 2003 dealt with the fact that, after the congressman mentioned in an early November forum that he was a bachelor, more than
eighty women contacted a New Hampshire website indicating that
they wanted to date him.

Kucinich was a good sport about the whole dating story. And,
certainly, there was nothing wrong with major media doing a feature
report on that quirky twist of the campaign trail. But there was something very wrong with the scenario where the story of his dating
habits was the big news about Kucinich while the story of his fight
against Diebold barely got notice.

Nothing so undermines the legitimacy of a presidential campaign in the months before the caucuses and primaries begin as the
denial of ongoing and thoughtful coverage. Over time, the media
sends the message that certain candidates are not to be taken seriously. And, in case anyone misses the subtle signal, it is sometimes delivered directly.

That happened in December 2003, when Ted Koppel steered
one of the most critical debates of the Democratic presidential contest toward horse-race questions about endorsements, poll positions,
and fund raising. The host of ABC-TV's *Nightline* made no secret of
his desire to silence Kucinich, Sharpton, and Moseley Braun, in what
might well have been the campaign's clearest act of media policing.
Koppel went into the debate with a set of questions deliberately de-

veloped in order to marginalize the trio of progressive candidates. According to the *Washington Post,* the *Nightline* host asked before the debate, "How did Dennis Kucinich and Al Sharpton and Carol Moseley Braun get into this thing? Nobody seems to know. Some candidates who are perceived as serious are gasping for air, and what little oxygen there is on the stage will be taken up by one-third of the people who do not have a snowball's chance in hell of winning the nomination."

That night, Koppel's over-the-top assault on the candidates he had decided should not be running created an all-too-rare opening for a serious discussion about what should be one of the most important issues in America today: media manipulation of the political process. And Kucinich did his best to seize that opening even though he knew it would not endear him to the reporters and editors who had already decided, albeit more quietly than Koppel, to pretend that his campaign did not exist.

The story of the Koppel-Kucinich clash began when the veteran newsman was selected as the moderator for the December debate in New Hampshire among the nine Democrats seeking their party's presidential nomination. The New Hampshire primary, the first in the country, was only a little more than a month away, and the debate was seen as a last opportunity to separate the wheat from the chaff. In theory, that is supposed to be done by party activists and voters who, after viewing the performances of the candidates, make the tough choices. In this case, however, Koppel had taken the task on himself, and it quickly became evident that the moderator had identified Kucinich, Sharpton, and Moseley Braun as chaff.

Koppel's decision to focus vast portions of the debate on horse-race questions and insider gossip about endorsements and polling figures rankled Kucinich, who had for some time objected to the neglect of his candidacy by most media. But it also did something else. By badgering Kucinich, Sharpton, and Moseley Braun with questions that suggested they should drop out of the race, Koppel exposed the dirty little secret of network television journalists who were covering the 2004 contest: With the news hole being squeezed by hyperventilating reports on celebrity sex and crime, there was little time left for covering politics. And broadcast reporters had, themselves, adjusted to the new constraints of bottom-line media. As such, they demanded a sound bite–driven contest between a handful of well-known candidates, rather than a wide-open competition with lots of candidates and lots of interesting ideas.

Decades of consolidation and dumbing down had created a reality that presented reporters with a stark choice: Keep coverage vapid or quit. As such, the policing process accelerated, not because the race, which had started earlier than ever, needed the heavy hand of Washington journalists shaping its progress, but because the media companies had placed budget and time constraints on democracy. Media managers had made it clear that covering a long, drawn-out nomination fight would be costly, and inconvenient. Covering a coronation, in contrast, was relatively cheap and undemanding.

They chose the coronation. And Koppel was dispatched to lop off the heads of the pretenders to the throne.

But, as is often the case with such intrigues, the execution proved to be a messier task than anticipated because the victims did not go willingly.

By seeming to complain about having to deal with such a large field of candidates, and by so expressly indicating which candidates he would like to see leave the competition, Koppel turned attention away from the contenders and toward the damage being done to American democracy by the self-serving calculations of the nation's television networks.

After gently poking Koppel for starting the debate with a round of questions regarding Al Gore's endorsement of former Vermont governor Howard Dean, Kucinich suggested that it was wrong to steer the debate toward process questions when fundamental issues such as the war in Iraq, trade policy, and national health care had gone unaddressed. Koppel shot back at Kucinich with a question about whether he, Sharpton, and Moseley Braun weren't really vanity candidates who would have to drop out because they had not raised as much money as other contenders. That's when the sparks flew.

"I want the American people to see where media takes politics in this country," the Ohio congressman replied. "We start talking about endorsements, now we're talking about polls and then talking about money. When you do that you don't have to talk about what's important to the American people."

The crowd at the New Hampshire debate erupted with loud and sustained applause. And Kucinich's campaign drew a response from around the country that was equally intense. Indeed, when it was revealed later in the week that ABC had made a formal decision to cut back on its already scant coverage of Kucinich, Sharpton, and Moseley Braun, activists barraged the network with e-mails, letters, and phone calls protesting the decision. Demonstrations were held outside ABC affiliates. Fairness & Accuracy In Reporting (FAIR), the nation's premier media-watchdog group, used Koppel's questions and ABC's decision to cut coverage of the three most progressive candidates to focus attention on the dismal failure of the television networks when it comes to taking politics seriously.

For his part, Kucinich did not simply bask in the show of sympathy for his plight. Rather, he used the controversy to focus attention on an issue with which he had long been associated: the fight to prevent media conglomerates from expanding their dominance of the discourse in American political and cultural life. Kucinich, who had worked in the past for the *Cleveland Plain Dealer* and *Wall Street Journal* newspapers, as well as a Cleveland television station, had been sounding the alarm for years about media monopoly and commercialism. An outspoken critic of the June 2003 move by the Federal Communications Commission to eliminate controls on media consolidation and monopoly, he was an ardent backer of efforts by Senator Byron Dorgan (D-North Dakota), Congressman Bernie Sanders (I-Vermont), and others in Congress to reverse the FCC rule changes and preserve media competition, diversity, and local content.

Turning the controversy over Koppel into what the late senator

Paul Wellstone used to refer to as "a teaching moment," Kucinich declared, "The response of the American people to the exchange between Ted Koppel and myself demonstrates that there is great concern about the proper role of the media in a democratic society. The American people clearly do not want the media to be in a position where they're determining which candidates ought to be considered for the presidency and which ought not to be considered for the presidency. Such practice by the media represents a tampering with the political process itself. The role of the media in this process has now become a national issue central to the question of who's running our country, and I intend to keep this issue before the American people, and I look forward to engaging America's news organizations as to what they might be able to do to be more responsive to the public concerns that are reflected in the powerful response to the issues I raised in the exchange with Ted Koppel."

Campaigning in Iowa several days later, Kucinich issued a detailed plan for reforming America's media that called for:

- Breaking up the major media conglomerates in order to encourage competition and quality as well as diversity. Kucinich called for limiting the number of media outlets one corporation can own in a given medium, such as radio, print, or television. He also proposed a ban on cross-ownership of newspapers, radio, and television in the same market by a single corporation.

- Expansion of funding for public broadcasting channels on television and radio, and expansion of support for community-controlled media, in order to ensure the existence of media outlets that are free of the influence of advertisers.

- Requiring broadcast and cable networks to provide substantial free air time for candidates and parties during election campaigns.

- Opening up the regulatory process so that citizens can

more easily challenge the licenses of local broadcast outlets that fail to provide local coverage and to direct coverage at the entire community they are supposed to serve.

- Permitting not-for-profit groups to obtain low-power FM radio station licenses. Kucinich sought to encourage the development of new, community-based, noncommercial broadcasting outlets.

- Withdrawal of the U.S. from the World Trade Organization. Media companies have been lobbying the WTO for the creation of policies that would allow trade sanctions against countries that limit foreign ownership of domestic media, establish standards for local content, and fund public broadcasting.

Kucinich even came up with an anti–sound bite sound bite: "I don't think ABC should be the first primary. The first primary should not be on a television network."

It was a good line, but not one that would make the evening news on ABC or the other networks. Despite the supposed diversity of broadcast and cable television options, none of the networks found time to report Kucinich's critique or his program—even though it touched on an issue, media policy, that members of Congress reported had provoked more calls, letters, and e-mails in 2003 from the American public than any subject except the invasion and occupation of Iraq. The decision had been made to ignore Kucinich.

DEAN CROSSES THE LINE INTO UNCHARTED TERRITORY

Howard Dean, the leader in the polls, was more difficult to dismiss, however. And he, too, had begun to talk about media monopoly.

Much was made in the coverage of the 2004 presidential campaign about the innovations Dean and his supporters brought to the process—from their prodigious on-line fund-raising operation to the embrace of the Internet as a tool for organizing "Meet-Ups," and for attracting huge crowds to early-in-the-season rallies. But one of the most interesting aspects of the Dean campaign was its embrace of the downright old-fashioned notion that issues—even complex issues involving global trade, health care reform, and, yes, media policy—could excite the electorate. Throughout 2003, Dean evolved rapidly as a candidate, transforming himself from a relatively predictable moderate governor of a small New England state into the unexpected tribune for millions of Americans who thought that the United States was headed in precisely the wrong direction. Dean got people listening with his criticism of the administration's rush to war with Iraq, but he built out his base of early backers by offering bold proposals for addressing issues that most prominent Democrats had avoided. That's what he did when he appeared at the Institute of Politics at the John F. Kennedy School of Government at Harvard University for a December 1, 2003 taping of the MSNBC program *Hardball with Chris Matthews,* which unexpectedly turned into the most serious discussion of media issues to be featured on a major network during the entire 2004 campaign.

Matthews asked Dean about the broad issue of deregulation, citing the examples of airline- and radio-ownership rule changes, and then asked, "Is that the wrong trend and would you reverse it?"

"I would reverse it in some areas," Dean replied. "First of all, eleven companies in this country control 90 percent of what ordinary people are able to read and watch on their television. That's wrong. We need to have a wide variety of opinions in every community. We don't have that because of [Federal Communications Commission chair] Michael Powell and what George Bush has tried to do to the FCC."

Dean did not have it exactly right. Measuring media concentration is controversial because there is debate over how broad the parameters should be, and, at any rate, Bush was merely extending policies that took shape under former President Bill Clinton. But his point was clear. And exciting. To his credit, Matthews leaped into the discussion, although he did so initially with an eye toward jabbing a competitor.

"Would you break up FOX?" asked Matthews. "Would you break it up? [FOX owner] Rupert Murdoch has *The Weekly Standard*. [He] has got a lot of other interests. [He] has got the *New York Post*. Would you break it up?"

"On ideological grounds, absolutely yes," Dean joked.

"No, seriously," Matthews said. "As a public policy, would you bring industrial policy to bear and break up these conglomerations of power?"

"The answer to that is yes," replied Dean. "I would say that there is too much penetration by single corporations in media markets all over this country. We need locally owned radio stations. There are only two or three radio stations left in the state of Vermont where you can get local news anymore. The rest of it is read and ripped from the AP."

Matthews pressed Dean. "So what are you going to do about it? You're going to be president of the United States, what are you going to do?"

"What I'm going to do is appoint people to the FCC that believe democracy depends on getting information from all portions of the political spectrum, not just one," Dean replied.

Matthews then asked Dean directly, "Are you going to break up the giant media enterprises in this country?"

"Yes, we're going to break up giant media enterprises," the candidate answered. "What we're going to do is say that media enterprises can't be as big as they are today. I don't think we actually have to break them up, which Teddy Roosevelt had to do with the leftovers from the McKinley administration."

Dean explained, "You have got to say that there has to be a limit as to how—if the state has an interest, which it does, in preserving democracy, then there has to be a limitation on how deeply the media companies can penetrate every single community. To the extent of even having two or three or four outlets in a single community, that kind of information control is not compatible with democracy."

As the crowd of Harvard students erupted with applause, a flustered Matthews asked, "How far would you go in terms of public policy? This is not—what you describe is not laissez-faire. It's not capitalism."

"It is capitalism," Dean shot back.

"How would you—what would you call it?" Matthews demanded.

"I am absolutely a capitalist," the candidate explained. "Capitalism is the greatest system that people have ever invented, because it takes advantage of bad traits, as well as our good traits, and turns them into productivity. But the essence of capitalism, which the right-wing never understands—it always baffles me—is, you got to have some rules. Imagine a hockey game with no rules. Nobody benefits. Nobody benefits. So you have got to have reasonable rules. And the rules have to protect everybody in the game."

The interchange was remarkable for several reasons. First, it occurred. The front-running candidate for the Democratic nomination for president incorporated the thinking of the burgeoning media-reform movement—which just weeks before had gathered for the first national conference on media reform in Madison, Wisconsin—into a discussion of deregulation. Second, Dean linked concerns about media consolidation to concerns about the health of American democracy. Third, he pointedly rejected the notion that regulation in the public interest is somehow un-American.

But, remarkable as Dean's comments may have been, they did not qualify as news in most U.S. media. In other countries—Britain, Canada, Australia, France, you name the location—if a leading contender for president or prime minister talked about breaking up "giant media enterprises," it would have been a major story. In the United States, it did not even garner serious coverage on MSNBC, let alone the other networks or the newspapers that were busy promising to cover the campaign better than one another.

They were too busy providing an illustration of what happens when the media set out to police the political process. The same media that had once treated the Dean campaign as a fascinating, if doomed, phenomenon, suddenly found that it was not doomed. And from there things went pretty much as *Time* magazine's Karen Tumulty predicted in an uncharacteristically forthright article published during the summer of 2003. "Look back at nearly every campaign trail to the White House, and you will find embedded in the asphalt the flattened form of a once-captivating outsider. The story line plays out as follows: He seizes the imagination with a compelling message and personality; he upsets the dynamic of the race; the media lavish attention and praise on him (there is talk that he has created a phenomenon that will change politics); he makes a rookie mistake or two under the TV lights; the reporters turn on him; his fanatical legions realize he wasn't the guy they thought he was; and finally his demise becomes part of the winner's heroic backstory." The trouble for the media was that Dean almost got too big to take down. Topping the polls and with endorsements coming his way from former Vice President Al Gore, the man who won the most votes in the 2000 presidential election, and other top Democrats, Dean began to look unstoppable. Democratic party insiders in Washington were scared; as, we later learned, was Karl Rove.

As it turned out, however, those fears proved to be unfounded, in large part because the media that had initially helped Dean achieve front-runner status was already hard at work taking that status away from him.

IT WASN'T THE SCREAM

In the fall of 2003 and the first weeks of 2004, well before the "I-Have-a-Scream" speech in Des Moines, a target had been painted on Howard Dean's back. "If you accept the horse race metaphor beloved by campaign pundits, it seems like the media looked to disqualify former Vermont governor Howard Dean even before he left the starting gate," explained FAIR's Peter Hart. Once thought to be a long-shot contender for the Democratic nomination, Dean found

himself anointed as the media front-runner weeks before any voters had their say. With that status came intense media scrutiny, much of it focused on Dean's perceived weaknesses. "Doubts About Dean: Behind the Democrats' Battle to Stop Him," declared the January 12, 2004, cover of *Newsweek.* The same week's *Time* probed the rise of a candidate who "barked and blustered," and who was originally thought to be "little more than entertainment value" to party insiders and the press corps. "Is the country willing to elect a Brahmin who grew up in East Hampton, N.Y., and on Park Avenue, who brings virtually no national-security experience to a post–9/11 nation and who governed a state that gives homosexuals all the rights that go with marriage?" the magazine asked.

Hart explained that, "Running against the party establishment is not a strategy likely to endear you to most political reporters, who view party insiders as their most valued sources and advisors. And Dean's coverage reflected this . . . [As] a Dean victory began to seem less and less unlikely, his press treatment got harsher: *Time's* Joe Klein wrote after an early debate that there was 'a critical decision the Democrats now face—between principled opposition to the Bush administration and populist demagoguery on the two main issues of this election, the war and the economy.' Dean, of course, represented the latter."

Suddenly, Dean's frankness, once celebrated as the antidote to the studied caution of John Kerry and the rehearsed populism of John Edwards, was treated as evidence of mental illness. A *Washington Post* headline, dismissing the former Vermont governor as a "Short-Fused Populist," ran above a news article that opened with the line: "Howard Dean was angry. Ropy veins popped out of his neck, blood rushed to his cheeks, and his eyes, normally blue-gray, flashed black, all dilated pupils." Dean's supporters were identified as "Deaniacs," who had "drunk the Kool-Aid"—a reference to the mass suicide of followers of the Reverend Jim Jones who in 1978 downed poisoned drinks at their prophet's behest—and *Newsweek's* Jonathan Alter declared that, "The greatest fear among certain Democrats is that if Dean does win the nomination, his liberal supporters will put their Birkenstocks on the gas pedal and drive the party right over the cliff." While it is not in any journalism job description that we have found, the media raced—with sirens blaring and lights flashing—to avert the crisis feared by the never-identified "certain Democrats." And, by the time of the first caucuses in Iowa, Dean had already been beaten down to size by coverage that did not merely seize on gaffes but that sought to create gaffes that did not exist.

An example of the latter phenomenon came on December 1, 2003, when Dean appeared on National Public Radio. The candidate was asked why he thought the Bush administration had sought to suppress information—including, it would later turn out, an August 6, 2001, intelligence briefing for the president, titled, "Bin Laden Determined to Attack Inside the United States"—regarding what the president knew about terrorist threats prior to the September 11, 2001, attacks on the World Trade Center and the Pentagon. The Democratic front-runner responded, "I don't know. There are many theories about it. The most interesting theory that I've heard so far— which is nothing more than a theory, it can't be proved—is that he was warned ahead of time by the Saudis. Now who knows what the real situation is?" As FAIR's Peter Hart notes, "Dean's point seemed obvious: Given the White House's unwillingness to provide complete disclosure to the commission, such theories will continue to float around." Yet, radio talk shows and cable television networks spun a story that Dean had said Bush knew the 9/11 attacks were coming and failed to act. Several weeks after the interview, CNN's Paula Zahn confronted Dean's campaign manager, Joe Trippi, with a demand that he explain his candidate's conspiracy theories. "Let me just repeat exactly what came off the transcript of the NPR radio show. And this is Governor Dean's remark, quote: 'The most interesting theory that I have heard so far,' he responded, quote: 'is that he was warned ahead of time by the Saudis.' " Tripp objected, saying that Zahn had left out Dean's dismissal of the speculation as "nothing more than a theory, it can't be proved" and the candidate's declaration that he did not know why the president was withholding information. Zahn was curt. "Well, I think our audience has a pretty good sense now of what was said and what wasn't said," Zahn declared. In fact, if they had only listened to Zahn, the audience would not have known what Dean had said, let alone his obvious intent.

One of the most bizarre and troubling assaults on Dean's then high-flying candidacy came early in November of 2003, after the Democrat told the *Des Moines Register* that, "I want to be the candidate for guys with Confederate flags in their pickup trucks."

For years, Democrats had been talking about how to reclaim "the

Bubba vote." That's a reference to white working-class men who, among other things, attach Confederate flag stickers to the back windows of their pickup trucks. The flags are usually situated next to stickers featuring the image of a little boy urinating on another brand of truck.

Perhaps Dean would have been better off if he'd said, "I want to be the candidate for Chevy drivers who are amused by the idea of taking a leak on Fords." But that would have started a whole different conversation. So he used a conventional shorthand of political insiders.

To hear his opponents and much of the media tell it, however, he might as well have said he wanted to be Strom Thurmond's running mate on the Dixiecrat ticket. Richard Gephardt claimed Dean was reaching out to voters "who disagree with us on bedrock Democratic values like civil rights." Joe Lieberman labeled Dean's comment "irresponsible and reckless." John Kerry said Dean was attempting to "pander to lovers of the Confederate flag." Wesley Clark said all candidates should "condemn the divisiveness the Confederate flag represents." And John Edwards, who made a big deal about going after the Bubba vote early in his campaign, grumbled that "to assume that Southerners who drive trucks would embrace this symbol is offensive."

Apparently Edwards, who then represented North Carolina in the Senate, had failed to look around many parking lots in his home region. Had he done so, he would have known that many Southerners who drive trucks do, indeed, embrace the controversial symbol, as do a lot of rural northerners with pickup trucks.

Neither Edwards nor any of the other candidates really believed that Dean, who was usually accused of being too much of a New England liberal to appeal to Southerners, was a Confederate flag-waving racist. They were just trying to create that impression. In doing so, they were being ridiculously cynical. And, of course, most of the media mirrored their cynicism by reporting on what came to be called the "flag flap."

What wasn't being reported was this reality: Every single presidential candidate who was expressing concern about Dean's remark had sat in meetings where political operatives, pollsters, and consultants discussed strategies for winning the votes of white working-class males. These voters, whose economic interests would be at least somewhat better served by Democratic policies but who tend to vote Republican for social and cultural reasons, have fueled the rise of the GOP in recent years. And Democrats have long been obsessed with figuring out how to reach them.

So why was the Dean comment controversial? Good question. It had something to do with the desperation of the other candidates, who at the time were having a hard time keeping up with the former Vermont governor's fund-raising juggernaut and burgeoning grassroots campaign. But it also had something to do with the collapse of basic journalistic standards in most major-media newsrooms.

Instead of pursuing the truth—or, at least, something akin to reality—the political reporters who picked up on the flag-flap story were practicing obeisance to power. They simply took down what candidates had to say and then published or broadcast it. Thus, when the other candidates tried to paint Dean as the reincarnation of Jefferson Davis, the media dutifully reported those absurd claims.

More responsible and engaged media would have stopped to ask the deeper questions: Why do so many white working-class males vote against their own economic interests? Is it because they are racists who really do embrace the Confederacy's legacy? Is it because the Democratic Party has so abandoned populist economic messages that even voters in what were once traditional Democratic constituencies have lost faith in the party and its candidates? The answers to these questions are complicated; but they are at the core of any serious examination of our politics.

Unfortunately, most politicians are unwilling to engage in real discussions about race and economics, let alone the complex zones in which they intersect. And as the controversy over Dean's comments illustrated, too many political reporters have lost the inclination, and perhaps even the ability, to demand better of politicians. In fact, in the role they have been forced to assume as the guardians of the status quo, most elite journalists have become the first line of defense against those who would shake things up.

After the media turned an innocent shout to his young supporters on the night of the Iowa caucuses into the scream heard 'round the world—again and again and again—Dean began to recognize the increasingly damaging role that a media warped by bottom-line pressures and entertainment values was playing in his own campaign and in the broader struggle to make real the promise of American democracy.

MISSING THE CHANCE TO MAKE MEDIA AN ISSUE

In a conversation during the last days of his campaign, Dean was frank about the crisis of American media, and about why he had not confronted it more aggressively.

"I think I scared them. I think it goes back to when Al Gore endorsed me, and AFSCME and the SEIU; people in the establishment began to think I could win," Dean said, recalling the heady days in the fall of 2003 when his insurgent campaign began to accumulate support from top Democrats and key labor unions. "That scared the hell out of them because they knew I didn't owe anybody. I didn't owe them a dime. Eighty-nine percent of our money comes from small donors. That's certainly not true of anybody else running for president on either side."

The "them" Dean was referring to are the Washington-based political pundits, commentators, and reporters who shape the discussion of presidential politics on television and on the pages of America's elite newspapers and on Sunday morning talk shows. "I think the media is part of the established group in Washington. They have a little club there," Dean explained. "If you don't go down to kiss the ring, they get upset by that. I don't play the game. I pretty much say what I think. That makes a lot of people uncomfortable."

Initially, Dean said, he felt he could take the hits. After all, media outlets that once dismissed him as the "asterisk" candidate from Vermont had helped to make him a national figure when they featured him on magazine covers and news shows during the fall. To an extent, he had to take the bad with the good.

But, after what he referred to as a "pep talk" to backers following his defeat in the Iowa caucuses began airing around-the-clock on cable news programs as the "I-Have-a-Scream" speech, Dean said he began to fully understand how events could be warped by the media.

"ABC actually did a fairly sound retraction on that one," Dean said of a report by ABC News that showed that the scream in Des Moines was dramatically amplified by the microphones used by television news crews covering the event. "But that's one network, and one report. Most of the networks failed to offer any perspective." (Long after the fact, CNN's general manager would also admit that the cable networks overplayed the scream.)

Dean was not whining. He did not suggest that he had run an error-free campaign. He admitted to plenty of mistakes. But he was suggesting that he had taken more than his share of hits in media coverage of the campaign's most critical stages. His complaint was confirmed by a report from the nonpartisan Center for Media and Public Affairs. The center's study of 187 CBS, NBC, and ABC evening news reports found that only 49 percent of all on-air evaluations of Dean in 2003 were positive. The other Democratic contenders collectively received 78 percent favorable coverage during the period.

In the week after what would turn out to be the definitional Iowa caucuses, the center found that only 39 percent of the coverage of Dean on network evening news programs was positive; in contrast, 86 percent of the coverage of Edwards was positive, as was 71 percent of the coverage of Kerry, the new front-runner.

After Iowa, of course, the coverage was dramatically more negative and dramatically more damaging for Dean. The scream aired 633 times on national networks in the four days after Iowa voted on January 19, thwarting attempts by Dean to renew his candidacy before the New Hampshire primary.

Even as he struggled in late January and early February to create a political resurrection, Dean did not talk much about media coverage of his campaign. Why? "It's not central to the stump speech. If I were leading the polls by 20 percent, I could say anything I wanted about the media," he explained. "But what I've discovered is that, if you complain about the media, they write that you're whiny and complaining. So I don't complain about the media."

That was a mistake. At a time when millions of Americans were taking up media issues, because of their general disgust with the coverage of the war in Iraq and the campaign for the presidency, and because of particular concerns about the FCC's moves to ease constraints on media consolidation, Dean should have gambled on opening a discussion with the American people about what the media was doing to him, and to democracy.

Unfortunately, the man who had come so close to beating the establishment was no longer in a gambling mood. "I figure I'll win," he gamely declared, "and then I'll really complain about the media," he said.

When we pressed him about what he would say, Dean displayed precisely the understanding of media and democracy issues that might well have made it possible for him to make an issue of media monopoly. He was not merely grumbling about bad coverage, he was talking about the structural issues that needed to be addressed.

"I think democracy fails under a variety of conditions and one of the conditions occurs when people don't have the ability to get the kind of information they need to make up their mind. Ideologically, I don't care much for FOX News. But the truth is that, as long as there are countervailing points of view available on the spectrum, it doesn't matter," said Dean. "Now, the last time I saw a statistic on this, I think that 90 percent of the American people got their news from a handful of corporations. That's not very good for democracy, and that's not very good for America. If I become president of the United States, I'm going to appoint a whole lot of different people to the FCC so that we start to make the media more diffuse, more responsible. I'd also like public airwaves devoted to some public services—so that every single station serves the community where it is located."

Dean dismissed the notion that proposals to break the grip of media conglomerates were particularly bold. "That's not radical at all," he said. "That's what we used to have. The right-wingers have undone that over the last fifteen or twenty years, and we need to go back to what we had to have a sound democracy."

Dean also dismissed the notion that it would be difficult to get the American people to support a challenge to big media. "I think the public would love what I was doing," he said of a presidential assault on media monopolies. "The public doesn't particularly like the media, which works in my favor."

But, of course, Dean never turned the discussion in his favor.

There are no guarantees that Dean could have changed the course of the campaign once more with an appeal to the American people's anger over media manipulation and irresponsibility. But he had so little to lose that it is tragic that he did not choose to throw down the gauntlet, perhaps with an homage to Howard Beale, the rabble-rousing anchorman of Paddy Chayefsky's 1976 film, *Network,* and to the candidate's own reputation for testiness: "I'm mad as hell and I'm not going to take it anymore!"

There is a postscript to the 2004 Democratic nomination campaign that should have made Dean even madder.

It happened that the New Hampshire primary results provided a case study for what might have been, a tiny entrée into a parallel universe where Howard Dean was actually treated responsibly by the media.

We are not talking about some Deaniac bizarro world where the former Vermont governor's "I-Have-a-Scream" speech would be treated as world-class oratory, or where it would go unmentioned that his campaign had squandered much of its cash reserve. We are talking about a place where Dean experienced the same treatment as the other candidates—criticized for his mistakes, complimented for his accomplishments, and, above all, treated seriously when he discussed issues.

How would a Dean candidacy have fared at key stages in the campaign if the press had gushed over him as it did John Edwards, or forgave him his trespasses as quickly as it did John Kerry, or overlooked the disorder in his organization as casually as it did the daily disaster that was Connecticut Senator Joe Lieberman's so-called campaign?

That's a no-brainer. Dean would have done better. The only question is "How much better?"

Before answering that question, certain stipulations must be made. For instance, Dean really did make a lot of mistakes on the campaign trail. And, of course, the media had a responsibility to report them. But there is simply no question that Dean's every misstep was amplified by a twenty-four-hour-a-day news cycle, by late-night comics, by an anybody-but-Dean army of cable television and talk-radio talking heads, and by Washington-centric newspaper columnists who never understood or particularly approved of Dean's decision to show up uninvited at the top of Democratic polls in late 2003. It wasn't just comics and commentators that gave Dean a hard time, however. As the nonpartisan Center for Media and Public Affairs noted, Dean was the favorite whipping boy of the evening news programs on the major networks even before the Iowa scream.

The battering Dean took from the media actually strengthened him at first in the late fall and early winter of 2003. Grassroots Democrats, like most Americans, were angry with media that did not have the courage—or the basic journalistic skills—to expose George Bush's lies about weapons of mass destruction and tax cuts for the rich before Americans started losing their lives in Iraq and their jobs in the heartland. For a time, the jabs he took from the media bounced off Dean as easily as did the attacks from the corporate-funded Dem-

ocratic Leadership Council and other fronts for the Republican-lite wing of the Democratic party. (As the campaign progressed, the media attacks and those of the DLC and the Republican National Committee began to parallel one another with increasing frequency.)

Ultimately, however, the hits took their toll. Despite the fact that Dean was actually better on his feet in the late stages of the campaign than at any time since he announced his candidacy, he was greeted with skepticism even by Democrats who admitted to preferring his message. In New Hampshire, Dean was still bringing crowds of Democrats to their feet with his antiwar, anti-establishment message. But when asked if they would support him, these same Democrats would quietly admit their intention to vote for Kerry, whose campaign had been plucked from the scrapheap of history by a strong showing in Iowa and a media pack that had suddenly determined he alone was "electable." Karl Rove did not believe the spin, but a lot of Democrats did.

Dean and his backers might grumble about reporters declaring the candidate to be the "dead man walking" of the 2004 campaign. But the results from the New Hampshire primary, in which he was once expected to confirm his viability, confirmed the diagnosis.

WHAT IF THE MEDIA HAD BEEN FAIR TO DEAN?

Just how much damage was done to Dean by the battering he took from a media that had determined he did not belong in the presidential race? After all, every disintegrating presidential candidacy since that of John Adams in 1800 has blamed the media for its decline. Where was the statistical proof of distinct damage done to Dean?

In southwest New Hampshire.

That region may have been the one corner on the campaign trail where Dean received good press—or, at least, fair press—right up to the time when ballots began to be cast. Southwest New Hampshire still gets a lot of its news from a feisty independent daily newspaper called the *Keene Sentinel*. Since 1799, the *Sentinel* has been synonymous with news in what is known as the Monadnock Region. The newspaper has a long history of taking politics seriously, and it still does. The *Sentinel* embodies what FCC Commissioner Michael Copps is talking about when he discusses the importance of "localism" in media—local ownership, local coverage, local perspectives. And, because of its unique location on the presidential campaign trail, every four years the *Keene Sentinel*'s local stories are those of the national campaign.

All the serious contenders for the Democratic presidential nomination campaigned aggressively in southwest New Hampshire, which borders Dean's Vermont and Kerry's Massachusetts. All of them earned front-page coverage of their statements and stands in the *Sentinel*. All of them sought the newspaper's endorsement.

So the Monadnock Region was treated to some of the most thorough coverage of the campaign in the country. And that coverage was not filtered through a news center in Washington or New York or Atlanta.

Thus, when it came time for the *Sentinel* to make an endorsement, the editors looked over their own coverage and came to a conclusion: Dean was not the screaming hothead portrayed on cable TV. Rather, they saw a sensible and appealing candidate, and they backed him, writing that, "Dean offers voters a wide range of well-thought-out policy initiatives, foreign and domestic, based on a dramatic—and one might say conservative—theme: I want my country back. That cry, coupled with Dean's direct, energetic style, appeals to a lot of Democrats and independents, and has attracted a large number of people to his campaign who had previously been alienated from politics of any kind. Dean is particularly effective in his open refusal to entice voters with wild promises of expensive new government programs . . .

"We come to this decision not without some difficulty, given the appeal of the . . . Clark and . . . Edwards candidacies. But we believe on balance that Dean is best-equipped to restore respect for this country abroad while protecting the interests of Americans at home. And we believe Dean, unlike the current occupant of the White House, understands that the two efforts must be linked. All nations reserve the right to act boldly in their own interests, but no nation— even our own exceptional nation—can thrive as a go-it-alone force on virtually every matter of international substance: energy, the environment, trade, war and peace. Dean has reasonable and we believe workable ideas for addressing Americans' needs regarding health care, the federal deficit, homeland security, jobs, civil rights and the economy. And he would reverse the current administration's shameless weakening of environmental laws.

"No one will accuse Howard Dean of being soft on anything—

that's hardly his style. But in the long run, tough policies are most effective when they are also smart policies. We observed Dean through a long career as governor of Vermont accomplishing a great deal by combining diligence with intelligence. Along the way, he usually won the respect not only of his allies, but of many of his adversaries as well. If he can bring that vitality and that sensitivity to the national stage, he and we might well get our country back."

The *Sentinel* wasn't the only thing Dean had going for him in southwest New Hampshire. But the steady and responsible coverage that the region's dominant newspaper accorded him, along with its endorsement, appear to have had some impact.

Kerry won New Hampshire by a margin of 39 percent to 26 percent for Dean. Dean, who had been leading in just about every New Hampshire region, according to polls taken late in 2003, saw his support slip dramatically in most places. But the former Vermont governor carried southwest New Hampshire, winning 6,639 votes to 6,070 for Kerry. Of thirty-one towns in the Monadnock Region, John Kerry won just eleven, while Howard Dean took twenty.

What does this tell us? We think it says that, more than anything John Kerry or Howard Dean did in 2004, the media coverage of the campaign is what mattered. Where the media beat the hell out of Dean, he was unable to withstand the blows. Where it gave him a fair shot, the story was a different one. We are not objecting to the media being tough on Dean. We think reporters and editors should be tough on all candidates. But, to our view, the record of the 2004 Democratic primary campaign is that of media going beyond toughness. A choice was made at a critical stage in the campaign, and that choice was to treat Howard Dean as a dangerous, perhaps unbalanced character, rather than a refreshing alternative to politics as usual. That was certainly how Karl Rove wanted Dean to be portrayed. We just wonder whether America really prefers a media that is so determined to police the process that it ends up doing Karl Rove's work for him.

CHAPTER 5

MEDIA AND THE NOVEMBER ELECTION

"God, they're doing the work of the Republican National Committee."

—John Kerry after taping a segment for ABC-TV's
Good Morning America, April 2004

John Kerry was uniquely ill-suited to be the presidential nominee of a major party in 2004. It was not that he was inexperienced; as a decorated military veteran, a former prosecutor, a former state official, and a twenty-year member of the U.S. Senate—where he had focused on international affairs, environmental issues, and the nation's fiscal health—he was arguably better prepared to assume the presidency than all but a handful of men who had sought the position in the course of the nation's history. Nor was it a matter of Kerry's failing to present himself as an able and generally acceptable replacement for an incumbent whose tenure had been characterized by serious questions of integrity and competence; indeed, if there was a criticism to be lodged against Kerry's campaign, it was that the candidate and his supporters tended to be too determined to appear, and in fact be, presidential. So why was Kerry ill-suited to the competition? Because he still believed that the American media was an independent, responsible Fourth Estate that could be trusted to cover the campaign fairly for the most part and that could be corrected, when it went astray, with a quiet call to a network executive or a newspaper editor.

Kerry's old-fashioned thinking with regard to the role that media play in contemporary democracy, while reasonably parallel to the perceptions of many older Americans, made him a painfully inept candidate in 2004. He played by rules that no longer exist, and he expected results that are no longer possible. It was not an issue of Kerry being out of touch with the new media of blogs and podcasts; all indications are that he understood the Internet, as a practical tool and as a potential force, far better than did George W. Bush. Rather, Kerry had never adapted to the radical changes in how a consolidated, formatted, and rigorously bottom-line oriented media covers politics. He did not understand that in most cases issues no longer mattered, that prevailing again and again in debates was inconsequential, and that having the truth on his side when he was attacked was about as useful as having a horse-and-buggy at the ready for a final campaign swing through the Midwest. John Kerry, who could not fathom that television networks and major newspapers would take seriously the mad ranting of the Swift Boat Veterans for Truth, lost the presidency because he clung throughout the campaign to the romantic notion that the media were still some sort of watchdog guarding against abuses of the political process rather than the vehicle by which the worst abuses were executed.

Kerry's misread is precisely the one that mainstream media seeks to perpetuate. In discussing the nature and outcome of the 2004 presidential election, prominent print and broadcast commentators have suggested many factors as being decisive: concerns about terrorism and moral values rank high on most lists. In our view, however, the only way to explain the bankrupt quality of the campaign and the outcome is the performance of news media themselves. We do not argue that it is a matter of journalists bending the stick in the direction of candidates they favor, although clearly Bush was the beneficiary of the media coverage. We argue that the issue is much more fundamental: There has been an utter collapse of credible political journalism in the United States to the point where powerful politicians are better positioned than ever to manipulate the coverage of campaigns, and citizens are left ill-equipped to participate in a meaningful manner in their own elections. And, as Bill Moyers reminds us, "the quality of democracy and the quality of journalism are deeply entwined."

While Kerry did not understand the full extent of the degeneration of American media, his opponent did. No American president since John Kennedy, the first to recognize the power of television, was so perfectly attuned to the media of his moment as was George W. Bush in 2004; and none since Theodore Roosevelt, who in another age saw the full potential of wire services and mass-circulation daily newspapers, was so willing to take advantage of opportunities for exploiting media in ways that his opponents could not begin to conceive. Few would suggest that George W. Bush was more media savvy than Kerry—indeed, the incumbent bragged that he did not read newspapers—and fewer still would suggest that the incumbent was more in touch with evolving technological developments than the gadget-obsessed challenger. In fact, Bush's advantage came not from experience or knowledge, but from his *lack* of experience and knowledge.

BUSH SAW MEDIA FOR WHAT IT WAS

Bush had no illusions about media. Where Kerry first came into contact with newspaper and television reporters as a young warrior-turned-protester in the early 1970s, who found that his story and his ideas were taken seriously and broadly disseminated by the nation's most respected journalists, Bush never really occupied the media spotlight until 1994. It was then that, as a candidate for governor of Texas, the son of a recently defeated president was taught by Karl Rove to distrust, disparage, and, above all, manipulate mainstream media while working closely with a burgeoning network of right-wing talk radio hosts to advance his candidacy and discredit his foes. Kerry's experience led him to respect mainstream media and to feel he could count on a measure of fairness and responsibility that no longer existed. Bush expected nothing from mainstream media except an empty balancing act that would treat any statement he made—no matter how absurd—as the equal of expressions from his opponents. The president had been taught to disrespect mainstream media and to believe—correctly, it turned out—that most major media outlets could be spun, threatened, and pressured into doing the bidding of his administration and his campaign.

Bush was lucky enough to assume the presidency at a point in history where the bottom-line of consolidated media had trumped all other considerations when it came to news coverage in general and political and government coverage in particular. "The State of the American News Media, 2005," which was produced by the Project for Excellence in Journalism, a research institute linked with the Columbia University Graduate School of Journalism and funded by the Pew Charitable Trusts, found that 37 percent of print, radio, and TV journalists surveyed cited cutbacks in their newsrooms during the run-up to the 2004 election cycle; and, amazingly, considering the rapidly increasing use of the World Wide Web as a source for news, 62 percent of Internet professionals reported cutbacks in their newsrooms during the period from 2002 to 2004. "For all that the number of outlets has grown, the number of people engaged in collecting original information has not," explained the report, which noted that investments in news operations tended to be directed toward repackaging and presenting information rather than news gathering. Most major media outlets no longer staff Washington bureaus with enough reporters to keep an eye on a presidential administration, the old days of assigning reporters to cover the vast majority of cabinet-level agencies are long gone, and with them the nuanced, ongoing coverage of issues relating to agriculture, labor, housing, and transportation. And they do not begin to have the staff needed to provide serious campaign coverage in a democracy where the population numbers almost three hundred million.

Even where major television networks and newspapers do staff Washington bureaus with a reasonable number of reporters, they tend to be celebrity journalists who are not about to risk the ire of the White House—or their bosses—by asking the tough questions that might get a journalist tossed off the official gravy train. These realities

meant that the Bush presidency rarely, if ever, faced the sort of scrutiny that past presidents have experienced. And after the September 11, 2001, terrorist attacks on the World Trade Center and the Pentagon, things got a whole lot easier for the commander-in-chief. It was during that time when the president and his aides perfected their relationship with U.S. mainstream media: The president relished the deference that was paid by reporters to the man who was supposedly leading a war on terror. And White House aides made it clear that the state of affairs would not be allowed to change. White House press secretary Ari Fleischer openly rebuked reporters and television personalities who were insufficiently patronizing—suggesting after 9/11 that the few dissenters left with forums, such as Bill Maher, the host of ABC-TV's *Politically Incorrect,* "need to watch what they say, watch what they do." The president stopped taking questions from veteran White House correspondent Helen Thomas, one of the few prominent reporters who kept pressing him, particularly on international issues. And the rest of the White House press corps, showing more concern about getting the right warm body for the next live shot than the independence of the Fourth Estate, accepted the banishment of Thomas.

Bush's aides were never naïve enough to believe that the United States has a liberal media, nor were they bothered by anecdotal studies that suggested coverage of Bush was more negative than positive at particular points during the campaign. They recognized that, while it is true that many reporters are liberals, their bosses tend to be classic corporate managers. And, as media has become more corporate—with ownership consolidating within companies that see journalism as a potential source of revenue, rather than a mission—the potential for newspaper, radio, and television news to stray beyond the comfort zone of the nation's economic elites has been dramatically reduced. While cultural conservatives may find legitimate grounds for complaint about sex, violence, and a general disregard for their moral values in particular publications, radio and television programs, books, and films, corporate conservatives have a lot less to complain about—particularly those employed by the military-industrial complex about which Dwight Eisenhower so presciently warned.

Still, a business-friendly media could not entirely neglect revelations regarding the administration's lies regarding weapons of mass destruction, scandals involving administration aides, sluggish job creation, and the burgeoning budget and trade deficits. Even for the most cautious reporters, it was difficult to ignore the concerns raised by some of the most successful business people in the country, including investment-guru Warren Buffett, about the wrong paths down which the administration was leading the nation. So, while the Bush team had few fears about being confronted by crusading liberal muckrakers who carried on in the tradition of the nation's greatest journalists, Rove and the other politically savvy strategists on the Bush team understood that incumbent presidents tend to face more scrutiny than their challengers. And, knowing Bush's vulnerabilities all too well, they set out to manage not just the questions but the questioners. David Shaw, the media critic of the *Los Angeles Times,* summed things up well when he observed that, "I don't think the president welcomes an inquiring press any more than he would welcome a congressional version of the Question Time to which the British Parliament regularly subjects the prime minister." Unlike British Prime Minister Tony Blair, however, Bush was able to manipulate pliant media into a position where inquiries were rare and quickly punished.

Bush never went to war with the media in the way that Blair did with the BBC when it began to report on how aides to the prime minister had "sexed up" intelligence data in order to make the case for war with Iraq. The American president and his aides recognized that decisions about how and what is covered by major media in the U.S. are made on a bottom-line basis. They knew that American media only rarely allows serious coverage of government or politics to interrupt the 24/7 slurry of celebrity scandal and entertainment that the television networks foist off on their viewers as news. Thus, the biggest favor the media did Bush in the 2004 campaign was simply to be itself. As Shaw noted, "The last time I checked, President Bush didn't dictate wall-to-wall coverage of Michael Jackson, Martha Stewart, Scott Peterson, and Chandra Levy." True enough, but he surely benefited from the diversion of public attention away from his actions as president and his campaign for a second term. An incumbent president, particularly a controversial one, gains an advantage when attention shifts from his foibles. And, again and again during the 2004 campaign season, the broadcast and cable networks, as well as many of the nation's largest newspapers, steered off the campaign trail and into the trials and traumas of the rich, the infamous, and the wholly irrelevant celebrities and criminals that are the main course in the diet of pablum fed the people in what can only be described as the post-modern era of American journalism.

THE PRESIDENTIAL PECKING ORDER

To the extent that major media outlets went through the motions of covering politics during the critical post-primary period when Kerry was defined in the eyes of American voters who did not live in Iowa, New Hampshire, or the handful of other key caucus and primary states that had been exposed to him, the coverage did the Democrat few favors. In the aftermath of the Democratic primaries, reporting on Kerry's campaign dropped dramatically, as most major media returned its focus to celebrity trials and scandals. Even when Kerry was covered, it was sparingly. According to a study by Media Tenor, the independent media institute, Kerry, who had received lavish and overwhelmingly friendly coverage during the late stages of the Democratic nominating process, saw his presence in leading national media outlets decrease to just 28.9 percent of the total political coverage during the spring of 2004. Al Gore's share of the coverage during the corresponding period four years earlier was 50.1 percent. In 2000, Gore and Bush received close to equal coverage in the postprimary, preconvention months. During the same period in 2004, Bush's media visibility was more than twice that of Kerry's.

As *Washington Post* media critic Howard Kurtz noted in July 2004, after the release of a report on newspaper, broadcast, and cable news coverage from the postprimary period by the Project for Excellence in Journalism, the Pew Research Center, and the University of Missouri journalism school, "The good news for President Bush is that he has dominated media coverage in recent months, a new study says. The bad news is that much of the reporting has focused on the president's character—and has been negative by more than a three-to-one margin. The bad news for John Kerry is that the media assessments of his character have been negative by a margin of more than five to one. The good news is he's been so overshadowed that there haven't been that many stories about him."

Coverage of the candidates and their campaigns would eventually even out as the parties staged their scripted conventions—four-day spin sessions organized entirely for campaign purposes—and the final push toward the November 2 vote began. Yet, even as the coverage grew more thorough and evenhanded, most media covered the election as another form of entertainment, focusing on the horse race, the clash of personalities and the manufactured scandals of Swift Boats, Rathergate, and whatever else came spewing out of Karl Rove's spin machine. Some of the media, mostly public broadcasting outlets and a handful of major daily newspapers, actually tried to cover the campaign as if the most powerful country in the world was going to elect its leader. But they were the exceptions to the rule of the picayune and sensational. Even the *Post*'s Kurtz, hardly a tough critic of consolidated media, admitted after the 2004 campaign that, "Big media corporations don't take a lot of risks, and entertainment drives a lot of today's coverage."

The Bush camp recognized that reality far better than did Kerry's crew. But that does not mean the president and his aides took anything for granted.

To assure that serious journalism did not become a problem for the president, the Bush administration established a model for how it would deal with mainstream media early on: Friendly media—the FOX News Network and other print and broadcast outlets owned by Rupert Murdoch's News Corp., Sinclair Broadcasting, the conservative newspaper the *Washington Times,* right-wing talk radio hosts, and individual reporters for local publications, broadcast outlets, and Internet sites that displayed an obvious pro-Bush bias—were lavished with attention. The rest of the media was treated respectfully, so long as it parroted the administration line, but was always kept at arm's length. And when a journalist strayed from the script—as Dan Rather of CBS News did during the fall campaign—there would be retribution. Indeed, the *New York Observer* reported that some CBS reporters only started getting calls returned from administration sources after Rather formally stepped down as anchor of the CBS Evening News program, months after the campaign was done.

In a broadcast media landscape organized as it currently is, with huge conglomerates pumping out a steady stream of random images that can loosely be referred to as news on a 24/7 basis, the demand for official sources—"talking heads with important-sounding titles," as one reporter put it—invariably overwhelms concerns about quality and content. Thus, networks compete with one another for the opportunity to be the first to report self-serving leaks from powerful insiders and to conduct vapid interviews with celebrity pols—the president, the vice president, key cabinet members such as former Secretary of State Colin Powell—rather than go after the sort of blockbuster news stories that cost substantial amounts of money to report and that run the risk of upsetting the nation's economic and political elites. Network news executives recognize that if they produce reports that offend the White House, they will have a harder time getting the coveted interviews and leaks that they crave. The Bush administration recognizes this as well, and during the 2004 campaign the Republicans artfully manipulated the television networks with an eye toward satisfying and starving the demand for soft news depending on the relative friendliness of the networks involved.

The president and his aides made little secret of their preferences among the networks. Vice President Dick Cheney, the dark prince regent of contemporary American politics, divides the journalistic community into two camps: "big-time" assholes (the phrase he used to describe veteran *New York Times* political writer Adam Clymer) and the favored employees of Australian-born media mogul Rupert Murdoch's far-flung empire. Murdoch's ideological organ, the *Weekly Standard,* may not have many readers outside the narrow circle of neoconservatives who still think the war in Iraq was a good idea. But it enjoys high circulation inside the White House. Editor William Kristol likes to suggest that the journal of uninspired imperialism has induced Cheney and others to embrace his publication's faith that America is ideally suited to fill the void left by the decline of the British Empire. Editors always like to imagine influences that may or may not exist. But, in this case, Kristol can point to solid evidence of Cheney's devotion to the *Standard's* vision. As he notes, "Dick Cheney does send someone to pick up thirty copies of the magazine every Monday."

Cheney is no elitist when it comes to Murdoch's products, however. A big viewer of the talk-television shows that clog cable systems with nightly conservative diatribes, Cheney delights in the programming on Murdoch's FOX News Channel. Indeed, he's a regular FOX aficionado.

Cheney, who in March of 2004 proudly noted that "my last full-blown press conference was when I was secretary of defense in April of 1991," may not have much time for most media. But Murdoch's FOX News Channel, the court reporter of the Bush administration, can always count on an interview, a leak, or, as happened in April of 2004, an official endorsement from the vice president. "What I do is try to focus on the elements of the press that I think do an effective job and try to be accurate in their portrayal of events," Cheney told Republican activists who were griping about the media. "For example, I end up spending a lot of time watching FOX News, because they're more accurate in my experience, in those events that I'm personally involved in, than many of the other outlets."

That Cheney sets the tone for the Bush administration on most issues is no secret, and this is certainly the case when it comes to relations with Murdoch. Indeed, the Bush administration's arm's-length relationship with most media during the run up to the 2004 election dissolved into a warm embrace whenever Murdoch called.

In mid-March 2004, during the week that marked the first anniversary of the U.S. invasion of Iraq, the Bush administration was busy pumping up hopes that its endless war on terrorism was finally going to yield a victory: the capture along the border between Pakistan and Afghanistan of the reputed Number 2 man in Osama bin

Laden's al Qaeda network. As it turned out, Dr. Ayman al-Zawahri was probably not among the militants holed up in the heavily fortified compounds that were being assaulted by Pakistani troops and their U.S. advisors.

But, by most measures, the prospective capture of what administration aides described as "a high-value target" was treated as a very big deal by the Bush White House. And that wasn't the only national-security issue that was in play. Administration aides were busy trying to hold together "the coalition of the sort-of willing" they had cobbled together to maintain the occupation of Iraq. With Spain's new prime minister declaring the occupation "a disaster" and threatening to withdraw that country's troops, and with Poland's president telling European reporters that his country was "misled" about the nature of the threat posed by Iraq, the administration had its hands full. Top Bush aides were also scrambling to counter charges by Richard Clarke, the former White House counterterrorism chief, whose book had caused something of a sensation by revealing that, prior to 9/11, the Bush team ignored "repeated warnings" about the threat posed by al Qaeda.

By any measure, National Security Adviser Condoleezza Rice, a key player on all the fronts that were exploding, had a very long list of responsibilities that week. Surely, she had no time for diversions, right? Wrong.

Rice took time out of the middle of the day on Friday, March 19, 2004, to address a secretive gathering that included Murdoch and top executives from television networks, newspapers, and other media properties owned by the media mogul's News Corp. conglomerate. Rice spoke at some length via satellite to Murdoch and his cronies, who had gathered at the posh Ritz Carlton Hotel in Cancun, Mexico.

Britain's *Guardian* newspaper, which sent reporter Lisa O'Carroll to Cancun, revealed that Rice was asked to address the group by executives of the Murdoch-controlled FOX broadcast and cable networks in the U.S. The FOX family of television networks and stations was accurately described by the *Guardian* as "hugely supportive of President George Bush."

"Although she is not there in person, the presence of Ms. Rice underlines the importance of Rupert Murdoch's news operations to the Bush administration, which may face growing criticism that it led the country into war on false pretences ahead of November's presidential election," the *Guardian* account of the Cancun gathering explained.

Of course, the relationship between News Corp. and the administration was a two-way street. In addition to FOX, Murdoch-controlled organs such as the *Weekly Standard* and the *New York Post* were always at the ready to spread the spin being peddled by administration aides. In return, Bush administration appointees to the Federal Communications Commission were making it possible for Murdoch's empire to rapidly expand operations in the U.S. In December 2003, the FCC approved News Corp.'s $6.6-billion takeover of DirecTV, the country's leading satellite television firm.

That decision made Murdoch the only media executive with satellite, cable, and broadcast assets in the U.S.

In other words, Rupert Murdoch is a very powerful player in the media, and—because of his willingness to turn his properties into mouthpieces for the administration—in the politics of the United States. So it should probably not come as any surprise that, like the politicians in any number of countries where Murdoch has come to dominate the discourse, Bush administration officials answer Rupert's call, even when they are supposedly preoccupied with national security concerns.

Yet, Rice's willingness to brief FOX executives was ironic in light of the fact that, at the same time she was entertaining the News Corp. executives, she was refusing to brief the bipartisan panel that was investigating the 9/11 terrorist attacks on the World Trade Center and the Pentagon. The National Commission on Terrorist Attacks Upon the United States would hear during that period from Central Intelligence Agency director George Tenet, Secretary of State Colin Powell and his predecessor, Madeleine Albright; Secretary of Defense Donald Rumsfeld and his predecessor, William Cohen; and President Bill Clinton's national security adviser, Sandy Berger. But Rice would, for weeks to come, steadfastly refuse to testify in public.

So it was that, when the National Commission on Terrorist Attacks Upon the United States called, the Bush administration's national security adviser was unavailable. But when Rupert Murdoch called, well, how could Condoleezza Rice refuse?

THE CODDLING OF THE PRESIDENT

During the course of the 2004 campaign, Bush would frequently make himself available for infomercial-style appearances with FOX News Channel personalities such as Bill O'Reilly and Sean Hannity. (O'Reilly began his grilling of the candidate in a September 27, 2004, interview by announcing, "I've got fifteen questions for you. If they're dumb, tell me they're dumb, because the audience will like that. If they're dumb questions say, 'Look, O'Reilly, that's just dumb.' "As it happens, Bush had no complaints about the intellectual depth of the questions.) But even when Bush sat down for a rare talk with an actual journalist, he tended to be treated with kid gloves, as when NBC-TV's Tom Brokaw asked if the president thought of himself as "a Ronald Reagan Republican." No, Bush replied, "(I) think of myself as a George W. Republican, different era." Laughs all around. End of interview.

Over time, Bush got used to the coddling. As the election year of 2004 was ramping up, a series of revelations shook the White House— the failure of the administration to respond to terrorist threats prior to 9/11, the obsession of Bush and his aides with attacking Iraq, the deliberate misreading of intelligence, and the dominant role in policy making that was played by Vice President Dick Cheney and Karl Rove all drew increased attention. But those stories were not dug up by reporters, and the president was rarely if ever questioned regarding them. Rather, the revelations were published in blockbuster books by ousted insiders such as former Secretary of the Treasury Paul O'Neill and former national security aide Richard Clarke. With budgets slashed and competition slackening, the White House press corps was no longer digging for news. Rather, it was waiting for news to happen, and even when a story did break out, broadcast reporters were agonizingly cautious in their questioning of a president who was known for his vindictive treatment of journalists who tossed anything more than the usual softballs.

Reporters from other countries were not so prone to the supine position as their American counterparts, however, as Bush learned in June 2004, when he was preparing for a fence-mending trip to Europe. It was then that Bush had an unpleasant run-in with a species he had not previously encountered with much frequency: a journalist. He did not react well to the experience.

Bush's minders had for the previous three years committed him to the gentle care of the White House press corps, which could always be counted on to ask him tough questions about baseball or when his summer vacation would begin.

Apparently under the mistaken assumption that reporters in the rest of the world were as ill-informed and pliable as those who cover the White House, Bush's aides scheduled a sit-down interview with Carole Coleman, Washington correspondent for RTE, the Irish public television network.

Coleman is a mainstream European journalist who has conducted interviews with top officials from a number of countries—her January 2004 interview with Secretary of State Colin Powell was solid enough to merit posting on the State Department's website.

But problems arose when Coleman, who apparently failed to receive the memo informing reporters that they are supposed to treat this president with kid gloves, confronted him as any serious journalist would a world leader.

She asked tough questions about the mounting death toll in Iraq, the failure of U.S. planning, and European opposition to the invasion and occupation. And when the president offered the sort of empty and listless answers that satisfy the White House press corps—at one point he mumbled, "My job is to do my job"—she tried to get him focused by asking precise follow-up questions.

The president complained five times during the course of the interview about the pointed nature of Coleman's questions and follow-ups—"Please, please, please, for a minute, OK?" the hapless Bush pleaded at one point, as he came close to begging his questioner to go easy on him.

After the interview was done, a Bush aide told the *Irish Independent* newspaper that the White House was concerned that Coleman had "overstepped the bounds of politeness." As punishment, the White House canceled an exclusive interview that had been arranged for RTE with First Lady Laura Bush.

Did Coleman step out of line? Of course not. Coleman was neither impolite nor inappropriate. She was merely treating Bush as European, Canadian, and Australian journalists treat prominent political players. In Western democracies such as Ireland, reporters and politicians understand that it is the job of journalists to hold leaders accountable.

The concept of accountability does not resonate with the American president. The chief executive, who so gleefully announced during the 2004 campaign that he did not read newspapers, had never tried to grasp the notion that journalists might have an important role to play in a democracy. And the hands-off approach of the White House press corps had reinforced Bush's conceits.

No doubt, Bush would have been well served during his first term by tougher questioning from American journalists, especially those who were working with the powerful television networks. And it goes without saying that more and better journalism would have been a healthy corrective for America's ailing democracy.

But the punitive treatment of Coleman and RTE only served to remind U.S. journalists that they had better not step out of line during the 2004 campaign. And for the most part, they did not.

SMOOTH SAILING ON SWIFT BOATS

The brief Q&A with Coleman was the president's last serious encounter with anything akin to aggressive journalism during the campaign season.

Effectively, it was smooth sailing from there on out. How smooth? Consider this: Despite the fact that most Americans expressed concerns regarding Bush's handling of domestic and foreign affairs, few specific issues ever earned the level of attention as did the faked debate about John Kerry's service in Vietnam. The role that the media played in making the fantastical discourse about whether Kerry deserved the medals he had earned while serving on a Navy Swift Boat in Southeast Asia one of the dominant issues of the fall campaign has been well established; indeed, the managers of the smear campaign openly boast about how, with a minimal investment, they forced the media to redefine the direction of campaign coverage.

Early in August 2004, following the Democratic National Convention finished in Boston, the so-called Swift Boat Veterans for Truth, a rag-tag band of conservative veterans who willingly served as props for an anti-Kerry smear campaign funded by White House allies from Texas, bought a small number of television ads attacking Kerry—immediately thereafter, right-wing Internet websites, along with conservative talk radio and cable television hosts began churning out daily reports on the charges. Soon, broadcast television outlets and daily newspapers were picking up on the controversy. As Dr. Kathleen Hall Jamieson, the director of the University of Pennsylvania's Annenberg Public Policy Center, explained in mid-August 2004, "The influence of this ad is a function not of paid exposure but of the ad's treatment in free media." Within ten days of the initial appearance of the Swift Boat commercial on a handful of stations in the battleground states of Wisconsin, Ohio, and West Virginia, a nationwide survey by the Annenberg Center found that 57 percent of Americans were aware of the commercial and the charges it made. A stunning 46 percent of those surveyed said they found the charges believable, and they weren't just partisan Republicans. According to the Annenberg Center's review, "Independent voters are nearly evenly split over whether they find the ad believable; 44 percent find the ad somewhat or very believable while 49 percent find the ad somewhat or very unbelievable."

Did this hurt Kerry? Undoubtedly. According to a survey conducted in nineteen battleground states in mid-August by the Republican polling firm of Fabrizio, McLaughlin & Associates (FMA), among likely voters who said the Swift Boat controversy was having an impact on their voting intentions, that impact was a negative for Kerry by nearly a three-to-one margin. "Make no mistake—controversy surrounding potential 'dirty laundry' still sells in American politics and this is a sterling example of it. But most surprising is that despite [Republican Senator John] McCain's swift and very public repudiation of this ad and the lingering questions on the veracity of the charges, it still ends up being a net negative for Kerry—especially among crucial undecided voters," explained Tony Fabrizio, a veteran political analyst who had served as chief pollster for Republican Bob Dole's 1996 presidential campaign. "In a close race where every little bit counts, Kerry can't afford to sustain too many minor hits like this."

But Kerry kept taking the hits, not merely from the Swift Boaters but from broadcast and cable media that—with their penchant for covering petty scandals and personality politics rather than real stories and real issues—gave Kerry's critics an open forum from the time Kerry was nominated until Election Day. Even after veteran Bush family retainer Benjamin L. Ginsberg resigned as national counsel to the Bush-Cheney reelection campaign in late August following the revelation of his connection to the Swift Boat group, many of the

nation's major broadcast and print media outlets continued to allow members of the organization to claim they were merely concerned veterans seeking to set the historical record straight. This "fair and balanced" approach to journalism fostered the lie that the Swift Boaters were credible players and gave the Bush campaign a tremendous boost—both by diverting the campaign from issues of the moment and by focusing the debate on Kerry's supposed character flaws. As the *Columbia Journalism Review*'s "Spin Buster" column noted during the campaign, "The [Swift Boat veterans] may have put themselves in the game, but it's a flawed media that made them stars."

143

Kerry certainly deserves a good measure of the blame for allowing the ungrounded and often bizarre charges of the Swift Boat Veterans to be taken seriously. Had he understood the modern media age a little better, he would have trumped the group immediately with a fiery denunciation of his critics for seeking to divert attention from Bush's draft avoidance with attacks on someone who volunteered for and actually shed blood in the Vietnam War. A media that does not like to pour resources into actual reporting loves a tit-for-tat that allows them to put talking heads on television; and when one of the talking heads is an angry veteran defending his honor the TV networks go wild. Kerry could have easily shut down the whole Swift Boat attack—thus undermining one of Rove's most carefully plotted strategies—if he had understood that major media in the United States no longer adds perspective to political discussions. But Kerry counted on the media to do the job that Jefferson and Madison had intended when they added a freedom of the press protection to the Constitution. That was a bad bet, which may well have cost Kerry the election.

Counting on the media to do its job was entirely in character for the Massachusetts senator who was similar in so many ways to the man he challenged for the presidency in 2004—both attended New England preparatory schools, both graduated from Yale, and both received advanced degrees from prestigious East Coast colleges—but who had developed dramatically different reading habits.

KERRY'S MISPLACED FAITH

Where Bush said he did not read newspapers, Kerry countered that he could not get enough of them. And that distinction, Kerry suggested when he sat down with one of the authors of this book for a rare extended interview on media issues in August of 2004, summed up a radically different vision of how a president should gather and process the information required to make fundamental decisions about the direction of the nation and the world.

"I read four or five papers a day if I can," said Kerry, when asked about his newspaper reading habits. "It depends obviously on where I am and what I'm doing. I always pick up a local paper in the hotel I'm staying at, or two depending on what the city is. And I try to get the *Washington Post, New York Times, Wall Street Journal, USA Today,* papers like that. I try to read as much as I can."

Kerry's reading habits were similar to most former presidents. Dwight Eisenhower read nine papers daily, Ronald Reagan was such an avid consumer of newspapers that his ex-wife Jane Wyman complained about his print media obsessions, and Presidents George H. W. Bush and Bill Clinton were known to go through stacks of papers each day. But Kerry's penchant for the papers clearly distinguished him from the current President Bush.

When asked in the fall of 2003 by FOX News anchor Brit Hume how he got his news, Bush said he asked an aide, "What's in the newspapers worth worrying about?" The president added that, "I glance at the headlines just to kind of [get] a flavor of what's moving. I rarely read the stories . . ."

Instead of gathering information himself, Bush said he preferred to "get briefed by people who probably read the news themselves" and "people on my staff who tell me what's happening in the world."

Kerry shook his head in disagreement as Bush's comments were recounted to him.

"I can't imagine being president and not reading as much as I can about what people are saying," explained Kerry. "I don't want [information] varnished by staff. I don't want it filtered by staff. I want it the way it is. And I think you get a much better sense of what's going in the country [when you gather information yourself]. I think one of the reasons we have some problems today is that we have an administration that's out of touch with the problems of average people. They don't know how people are struggling. They don't know what's happening with health care, employment. They don't know, or they don't care, that's their choice."

As a constant consumer of news, Kerry said he spent a good deal of time thinking about the role of media in a democratic society. And he admitted that he got frustrated when television networks and stations failed to live up to the responsibilities that should go with their colonization of the people's airwaves.

When it was mentioned that many Americans had expressed disappointment with the decision of the nation's broadcast television networks to air only three hours of coverage of the Democratic National Convention, Kerry said, "I share the disappointment. We're a democracy, and the strength of our democracy is in the ability of citizens to be informed.

"If the major media are unwilling to inform—and simply because there is not a clash or a conflict or something doesn't mean [a convention] is not informative—I personally think it's a derogation of their responsibility [that goes with using] the broadcast airwaves." In particular, Kerry said he was upset that the nation's commercial broadcast networks—including ABC, CBS, and NBC—decided not to air any coverage on the second night of the convention in Boston. That was the night when Illinois U.S. Senate candidate Barack Obama delivered a much-praised keynote address, Ron Reagan broke ranks with the Republican Party to criticize President Bush's limits on stem-cell research, and Teresa Heinz Kerry spoke about her husband.

"My wife gave a wonderful speech, Ronald Reagan, Barack Obama, it was a brilliant night," said Kerry. "I think it's very disappointing that the American people, at least the people who watch the networks, missed it. I talked to several of the anchors beforehand but, you know, that's the way they decided. Obviously, I disagreed."

Asked if he thought the decision of the networks to downplay the coverage of the convention sent a signal that told Americans not to take what happened in Boston seriously, Kerry said, "I don't know if it's that message or not. I think most Americans are smart enough to understand [that it does matter]."

But Teresa Heinz Kerry, who was seated next to her husband, interrupted him and said, "That is the message, I think. I agree that it hurts."

Concerns about consolidated media, particularly consolidated media that does not see itself as having a responsibility to cover politics seriously and to question those in positions of authority, had been highlighted that summer in documentaries such as Robert Greenwald's *Outfoxed,* a critique of the conservative bias of Rupert Murdoch and his FOX News programs, and Michael Moore's *Fahrenheit 9/11.* But Kerry had not yet seen either film and, while he marveled at their "remarkable" success, he remained relatively cautious about embracing the critique both films made of U.S. media. "I'm against the ongoing push for media consolidation. It's contrary to the stronger interests of the country," said Kerry, who added that diversity of media ownership and content was "critical to who we are as a free people. It's critical to our democracy."

But, aside from one speech in August to minority journalists, Kerry never really made an issue of media consolidation or the degeneration of the political debate that goes with it. That was a critical mistake for the Democratic nominee, who was uniquely positioned to force a dialogue about media that would have aided not just American democracy but his own campaign. Every four years in the United States, the nominees of the two major political parties are afforded the best bully pulpits that the nation has to offer. Used properly, these platforms offer candidates—particularly challengers—an all-too-rare opportunity to shine light on unaddressed concerns, add new issues to the debate and, ultimately, reframe the discourse. It is an awesome power, especially in an era when the words of U.S. presidential candidates are amplified not just nationwide but worldwide.

Unfortunately, Kerry did not use his bully pulpit wisely. Instead of aggressively pointing out that the media was parroting Bush campaign spin and strategies—not merely with regard to the Swift Boat controversy but with the general frame of a fall campaign where the national security issues favored by Karl Rove and the Bush team took precedence over the economic issues that were more likely to benefit the Democrats—Kerry chose to avoid blunt challenges to what may well be the primary pathology of the political moment. Now and again, Kerry would blow up, as he did when ABC-TV's Charlie Gibson based a line of questioning on widely-circulated Republican National Committee (RNC) talking points, a frequent practice even of the country's most prominent broadcast journalists. "God, they're doing the work of the Republican National Committee," Kerry grumbled, after the interview finished. Had he done so while the cameras were on, he might have sparked a necessary discussion about the collapse of journalism and the over-reliance by reporters on talking points and other forms of spin produced by the burgeoning opposition research programs of both major parties.

But Kerry always opted for the outdated approach of quietly rebuking an interviewer off camera, expressing his concern to a network anchor or chatting up an executive while vacationing on Martha's Vineyard. (Don't forget that media companies spread their money around the political field. As Sakura Saunders and Ben Clarke noted in a CorpWatch report on campaign giving by media companies, "Two of Kerry's top four career [campaign-funding] patrons are the law firms Mintz, Levin, Cohn, Ferris, Glovsky and Popeo, who represent telecom and cable interests, and Skadden, Arps, Slate, Meagher & Flom, who represent Time Warner and News Corp. Time Warner also ranks in the top four category of Kerry supporters.") The problem is that off-camera interventions have little impact on journalists, editors, anchors, and executives who are merely cogs in rigorously formatted money-making machines. Whatever the reason for Kerry's reticence, it cost him politically. The only way Kerry could have shaken the system in 2004 was by using the bully pulpit to speak publicly, and constantly, about the failures of the media. By failing to do so, he accepted a framework, and a set of rules of engagement, that favored Bush at every turn. To the very end, the Democratic nominee seemed to believe that the better angels of mass media would ultimately set things right. Only after the election was done did Kerry seem to fully recognize the reality of what hit him in the fall of 2004.

"There has been a profound and negative change in the relationship of America's media with the American people," Kerry told a March 2005 gathering at Harvard University's Kennedy School. "If 77 percent of the people who voted for George Bush on Election Day believed weapons of mass destruction had been found in Iraq—as they did—and 77 percent of the people who voted for him believed that Saddam Hussein was responsible for 9/11—as they did—then something has happened in the way in which we are talking to each other and who is arbitrating the truth in American politics. . . . When fear is dominating the discussion and when there are false choices presented and there is no arbitrator, we have a problem."

For the most part, Kerry assessed the problem correctly. "The corporatization of the media in America has taken away some of the willingness of the media to do the great muckraking they used to do periodically and to demand accountability of the powerful. And so you have so many different media outlets that are just bottom-line, and they go where the ratings tell them to go," the senator explained. "And there's a top-down hierarchical administration of what they'll go after and what they'll do, and it's driven by the economics more than anything. I think if we were to change the economics a little bit through grassroots effort, then you might begin to see a shift." But Kerry betrayed his lingering naïveté when he said, "We learned that the mainstream media, over the course of the last year, did a pretty good job of discerning. But there's a subculture and a sub-media that talks and keeps things going for entertainment purposes rather than for the flow of information. And that has a profound impact and undermines what we call the mainstream media of the country. And so the decision-making ability of the American electorate has been profoundly impacted as a consequence of that. The question is, what are we going to do about it?"

THE BLOGGING OF DAN RATHER

Kerry did not go into a lot of detail regarding the "sub-media." But no one doubted that he was referring to conservative blogs on the Internet, along with the right-wing talk-radio hosts who dogged him throughout the campaign on everything from his Vietnam record to his supposedly French demeanor. There's no question that Kerry took his hits from the Right's media machine. But there's also no question that he was helped by progressive blogs and liberal talk-radio hosts such as Al Franken on the Air America network that came into being during the 2004 campaign. For the most part, blogs preach to the converted, creating super-informed activists on the Left and Right but doing little to grow the bases of those ideological movements. Talk radio stretches the boundaries of the discourse a bit, but not nearly so far as fans of the format suggest. Television news programs—along with the ads that are run in so-called battleground states—remain the dominant sources of information about politics, followed by daily newspapers. Most Americans are not supercitizens. They do not hunt down detailed backgrounder reports about candidates or issues. They rely on mainstream media to provide them with the basic information they need to make informed decisions. Thus, the significance of new media in the 2004 campaign was less as an information source for voters than as a prod and punisher for old media. Former *New Yorker* editor Tina Brown got it half right when she belittled "the conventional wisdom . . . that the media will be kept honest and decent by an army of incorruptible amateur gumshoes" tapping away on their laptops. "In fact," Brown pointed out, "cyberspace is populated by a coalition of political obsessives and pundits on speed who get it wrong as much as they get it right. It's just that they type so much they are bound to nail a story from time to time." The part she missed was the fact that right-wing bloggers, often working hand in hand with GOP operatives, developed a remarkable talent for scaring mainstream media off big stories about Bush.

That became painfully obvious when the conservative bloggers went after the one network television anchorman who actually tried to engage in a little bit of journalism during the 2004 campaign. Plenty of ink has been spilled on the whole "Rathergate" controversy that developed after veteran CBS anchor Dan Rather attempted to unravel the mysteries of Bush's National Guard service during the Vietnam War. Rather blew the story, badly, and he got called on his missteps immediately by conservative bloggers who raised damning questions about the reliability of the documents on which Rather based his report that Bush got preferential treatment at a time when other men his age were being sent to their deaths in Southeast Asia. The slow cuts of the bloggers bled the life out of Rather's story and what was left of his career as a journalist. But they never succeeded in discrediting the basic assertion that Bush used his connections to avoid serving in Vietnam—first by gaining a coveted National Guard slot and then by getting special treatment when he failed to show up for required exercises. That did not matter, however, because the bloggers had effectively intimidated CBS and the rest of the media into letting the investigation go cold.

One of the few sensible voices in the whole controversy over the documents CBS News used in its ham-handed attempt to raise questions about Bush's service in the Texas Air National Guard came from retired typist Marian Carr Knox. As a former assistant to the late Lt. Colonel Jerry Killian, Bush's squadron commander who allegedly suggested that officers had been pressured to sugarcoat their evaluations of the politically connected young guardsman, Knox was in a position to know more than just about anyone else about the authenticity of the documents and the sentiments expressed in them. In interviews with several news outlets, including CBS, Knox suggested that the Killian memos were forged but accurate.

After Rather had acknowledged that he made a "mistake in judgment" when he relied on dubious documents for the *60 Minutes* report that detailed some of the favorable treatment Bush received, Knox's seemingly strange statement offered one of the few realistic

routes out of the thicket of spin the Bush administration and its blog-
ging brigades erected to avoid a serious discussion of the president's
failure to do his duty during the great war of his youth.

Knox said she did not think the memos that were purported to
have been written by Killian were genuine. But, she said, they reflected sentiments the National Guard commander expressed at the
time. Thus, the documents that caused a high-profile controversy as
the 2004 presidential campaign entered its final weeks could indeed
have been both forged and accurate.

So where should Knox's insight have led journalists and all those
Americans who rely on them for information?

First, anyone who wanted to know the truth about Bush's pam-
pered service should have been furious with Rather and the CBS
crew. When they failed to follow basic fact-checking standards, they
failed viewers who were, for the first time in a national broadcast context, exposed by the September 8, 2004, *60 Minutes* broadcast to a
seemingly serious review of irregularities related to Bush's entry into
the guard, his ignoring of direct orders, his failure to show up for
duty, and a pattern of reassignments that seemed always to benefit the
son of a then congressman from Texas rather than the country he was
supposed to be serving.

After more than a month of virtually round-the-clock assessment
of Kerry's Vietnam service, major media outlets had a responsibility
to reexamine the president's controversial service record.

Yet, by doing a haphazard job of reporting and then rushing to
broadcast the supposed blockbuster story, Rather and his crew played
into the hands of a Bush spin machine that was exceptionally adept at
peddling the lie that a liberal media was out to distort the president's
record. While their intent may have been to shed light on an interesting and potentially significant story of the special treatment accorded
this son of privilege, Rather and CBS, in their search for a scoop, created a fog so thick that it obscured the story for the rest of the campaign.

By relying on a few documents that were not adequately verified, CBS handed Rove's Republican spin machine exactly the diversion it needed to steer attention away from the real story. Of course it remains true that, as Rather said, "Those who have criticized aspects of our story have never criticized the heart of it . . . that George Bush received preferential treatment to get into the National Guard and, once there, failed to satisfy the requirements of his service."

Unfortunately, the heart of the story was ripped out of the public dialogue by the controversy over the doctored documents.

In the end, Rather and CBS were guilty of undermining not just their own story but the truth. That was particularly tragic because it was never really their story in the first place. The basic report of the machinations that George Herbert Walker Bush performed to help his son avoid serving in Vietnam, and the dirty details of the son's failure to do his duty as a guardsman, had been confirmed almost five years earlier by Texas columnist Molly Ivins and Texas investigative reporter Lou Dubose in their still-essential assessment of young Bush's path to power, *Shrub: The Short But Happy Political Life of George W. Bush*. That book's chapter regarding Bush's Vietnam-era Guard duty was exceptionally well-reported, compelling, and, ultimately, more damning of the Bush family and the current president than anything produced since its publication.

So why didn't Rather and the CBS crew simply invite Ivins and Dubose, both experienced Texas reporters with long histories of sorting fact from fiction when dealing with the Bush family, to help produce a *60 Minutes*–like report that would have told the story accurately and thoroughly? CBS executives apparently feared that, because Ivins and Dubose wrote with a point of view, rather than feigning journalistic impartiality, they could not be trusted to get the story straight. That, of course, is a common bias of the elite broadcast media in the United States.

Unfortunately, that bias led Rather and CBS to produce a story that did severe damage to prospects that the great mass of Americans would ever learn the truth about their president's Vietnam-era service. There is a lesson to be learned here: There was never any need for Rather and CBS to go searching for a scoop regarding Bush's time in the Guard. What there was a need for was a network with the courage to take that story, attach some pictures, and broadcast it. Unfortunately, CBS proved incapable of performing that simple task. And, in so doing, the network that did so much to define American television news in the days when Walter Cronkite occupied the anchor chair, put the truth a little further out of reach for most Americans.

Within a week after the Rathergate controversy blew up, CBS hung up its journalistic spurs.

The late-September decision of the network to delay the broadcast of an investigation into how the Bush administration manipulated intelligence and played upon fears in order to make the case for war with Iraq was the single most unsettling development in a political year that had been defined by unsettling moments. CBS News officials, rocked by Rathergate, announced that they would wait until after the November 2 election to broadcast the much-anticipated investigation of the steps the administration took to warp the debate about whether to go to war.

The fear, at least as it was officially expressed by CBS, was that revealing the extent of the administration's misdeeds might influence the outcome of the election by letting the American people in on what had really been going on in Washington. Thus, a CBS statement announced, "We now believe it would be inappropriate to air the report so close to the presidential election."

Critics were quick to suggest that the decision had less to do with a desire to be fair and balanced than with fear on the part of CBS corporate honchos that the airing of the exposé would provoke another round of charges that the network was displaying anti-Bush bias. Still reeling from the doctored-documents fiasco, CBS insiders quietly admitted that they were afraid to broadcast reports about the doctored documents the Bush administration used to make its case for war. Critics also noted that Sumner Redstone, CEO of CBS's parent company Viacom, had repeatedly suggested in public statements and interviews that "from a Viacom standpoint, we believe the election of a Republican administration is better for our company."

But let's put these legitimate concerns aside and accept CBS at its word.

Let's accept that the network did not want to air the report before the election because of genuine concerns on the part of CBS News professionals and CBS corporate officials about what impact sharing the truth with the American people might have on voting patterns.

Then we can be clear about what happened in the fall of 2004: CBS News ceased to be a news organization.

A network that worries about whether its reports will offend the people who are in power is no longer practicing journalism. And a network that is so worried about being accused of bias that it will not reveal the truth to its viewers is no longer in the business of distributing news.

Jefferson, Madison, and the other founders of this country created the framework for a free press, and fought mightily to defend the rights of dissident editors in the first years of the republic, because they feared the abuses of power that would result if presidents went unchallenged. They knew that democracy would only function if independent watchdogs were forever barking at the powerful from the columns of the partisan newspapers of their day. Jefferson may have put it best when he wrote in 1816 that, "The functionaries of every government have propensities to command at will the liberty and property of their constituents. There is no safe deposit for these but with the people themselves, nor can they be safe with them without information. Where the press is free, and every man able to read, all is safe."

By extension, when powerful media outlets censor themselves, the safety to which Jefferson referred is threatened.

The notion that a journalist would sit on a story because he or she fears being accused of bias, or because an exposé might have an impact on a presidential election, would have shocked and offended

Jefferson, Madison, Tom Paine, and the others who fought at the start of this American experiment to forge the way for a free press.

If ever there was a time when a bold and unyielding free press was needed, Jefferson had explained two centuries earlier, it was on the eve of a national election. At the point when the American people are preparing to determine who will lead their country, they need more than just stenography. They need news outlets that seek, without fear or favor, to speak truth to power.

Without a free flow of information, especially controversial and shocking information about the most pressing issues of the day, citizens cannot make informed choices. And when citizens cannot make informed choices, democracy ceases to function. With their decision to sit on a story of how the Bush administration manipulated this country into war, CBS News officials chose to block the free flow of information. As such, they broke faith with the promise of a free press. They became mere stenographers to power, and impediments to democracy.

Sadly, CBS, while more egregious in its actions than other networks, was anything but an anomaly in a year when few journalists chose to live dangerously.

NO DEBATE

When no other network picked up the threads of the story about Bush's Vietnam service or his manipulation of intelligence prior to the invasion of Iraq, the president was free to enter into a series of so-called debates where pressure to sacrifice the truth in order to appear fair and balanced—and the ridiculous reliance on confirmed partisans as commentators—meant that the American media generally avoided expressing the blunt assessment of international observers: that Bush lost all three confrontations with Kerry. Of course, the American people were the real losers. They never got to view real debates involving the candidates for president. Instead, they witnessed

THIS MODERN WORLD

by TOM TOMORROW

Panel 1: CBS THINKS IT HAS A NEW ANGLE ON AN OLD STORY. WE HAVE OBTAINED A **BAR TAB** RUN UP BY GEORGE W. BUSH IN 1967--**PROVING** THE PRESIDENT WAS ONCE A **DRUNKEN FRAT BOY!**

IT'S A **SCOOP**, I TELL YOU--A **SCOOP!!**

Panel 2: BUT **SOME GUY WITH A WEBSITE*** QUICKLY NOTES A **DISCREPANCY!**

SOMEONE HAS DOODLED A SEVENTIES-ERA "SMILEY FACE" ON ONE CORNER OF THE BAR TAB! **NO ONE** WAS DOODLING THE "SMILEY FACE" IN 1967!

THIS BAR TAB IS A **FAKE!**

*"SOME GUY WITH A WEBSITE." © AUGUST POLLAK, WWW.XOVERBOARD.COM!

Panel 3: THE POSSIBILITY OF FORGERY SOON **DOMINATES** THE STORY!

UP NEXT, WE DEBATE THE **MOST IMPORTANT ISSUE** OF CAMPAIGN 2004--

--WHEN **DID** PEOPLE FIRST START DOODLING "SMILEY FACES"?

Panel 4: CBS IS ULTIMATELY FORCED TO ISSUE A RETRACTION.

THE DOCUMENT WAS FAXED TO US BY SOMEBODY WHO KNEW SOMEBODY WHO SAID HIS UNCLE USED TO BE A **BARTENDER!**

HOW WERE **WE** SUPPOSED TO KNOW IT WASN'T GENUINE?

Panel 5: THE WHITE HOUSE RESPONDS WITH **INDIGNATION!**

THERE ARE **QUESTIONS** WHICH NEED TO BE **ANSWERED!**

BY **CBS**, I MEAN! NOT BY **ME!**

NO UNANSWERED QUESTIONS **HERE**, NOSIREE!

GO AWAY NOW.

Panel 6: GUYS WITH WEBSITES CAN'T STOP PATTING THEMSELVES ON THE BACK.

HAH! CBS MADE A **MISTAKE**--AND **WE CAUGHT THEM!** CAN THERE BE ANY DOUBT THAT THE **ENTIRE NEWS MEDIA** WILL SOON BE REPLACED BY **GUYS WITH WEBSITES?**

I THINK **NOT.**

Panel 7: QUESTIONS ABOUT THE PRESIDENT'S PAST ARE APPARENTLY **FORGOTTEN.**

HECK--IF THAT BAR TAB WAS A **FORGERY**, IT CLEARLY PROVES THAT **NO** YALIE **EVER** DRANK TO EXCESS!

I THINK IT PROVES THAT THERE ARE **NO DRINKING ESTABLISHMENTS** IN **NEW HAVEN!**

Panel 8: AND SOMEWHERE, KARL ROVE SMILES.

GEE, KARL--THIS COULDN'T HAVE WORKED OUT BETTER IF YOU'D PLANTED THAT BAR TAB **YOURSELF!**

YES, WELL--WE MUSTN'T QUESTION OUR GOOD FORTUNE, SIR.

TOM TOMORROW © 2004 ... www.thismodernworld.com

---

joint public appearances by the major-party contenders, which had been organized along lines dictated by the former Democratic and Republican party chairs who head the corrupt Commission on Presidential Debates, the campaigns, and the television networks that are willing accomplices in the lie that these events are real debates. Much of the criticism of the forums in recent years has focused on the exclusion of third-party candidates—an entirely legitimate complaint—but of equal concern should be the exclusion of diverse journalistic voices. For all the hype of the networks, the softball questions and deferential approach to the candidates on display in the debates make them appear more like broadcasts of discussions in the Supreme Soviet than decisive moments in a functioning democracy. A review of the three presidential debates that aired in the fall of 2004, and of the spin-drenched coverage of them, would lead any honest observer to share the conclusion of John Anderson, the former Republican congressman and presidential candidate: "The Commission on Presidential Debates must be replaced if we want to have a democracy in this country." Unfortunately, while a few newspaper editorial pages echoed Anderson's call, the broadcast and cable television networks confirmed their inadequacy by facilitating the commission's misdeeds.

What was striking about the debates was the extent to which the candidates, as opposed to their questioners, guided the discussion. Because they had both supported the war, Bush and Kerry were not asked basic questions about its morality, legality, or wisdom. Instead, they were generally asked tactical questions about how they would pursue the endeavor. Contrast that with the British elections of May 2005, which pitted Prime Minister Tony Blair's Labour Party against Michael Howard's Conservative Party. Howard had supported Blair's push for Britain to join George W. Bush's Coalition of the Willing, and neither man wanted to make the war an issue. Yet, smaller parties and the media refused to play by the Blair-Howard script. Rather, they continued to ask probing questions about whether Blair had failed to share important information regarding the legality of the war with his cabinet and the Parliament. Finally, Blair was forced, less than two weeks before the election, to release previously secret details of the pre-invasion internal debate over whether or not Britain should enter the war. On April 25, 2004, the *New York Times* headlined a report from London, "With 10 Days to British Vote, War Emerges As Top Issue."

The three presidential debates of 2004 in the United States inspired no such headlines in the *New York Times*. Nor, as it happened, did the most intriguing discussion to come out of the debates. That discussion involved the speculation about whether or not Bush used a listening device in order to get prompts from Rove and other aides during the first debate. As FAIR revealed in an investigative article, "Emperor's New Hump," which appeared in its journal *Extra!,* major media outlets shied away from seriously examining evidence that Bush "had worn an electronic cueing device in his ear and probably cheated during the presidential debates." Though the clear hump that was seen beneath Bush's jacket during the first debate gained mention in the monologues of Jay Leno, David Letterman, Jon Stewart, and in cartoonist Garry Trudeau's "Doonesbury" strip, salon.com writer Dave Lindorff noted in the *Extra!* piece: "That the story hadn't gotten more serious treatment in the mainstream press was largely thanks to a well-organized media effort by the Bush White House and the Bush/Cheney campaign to label those who attempted to investigate the bulge as 'conspiracy buffs.' In an era of pinched budgets and an equally pinched notion of the role of the Fourth Estate, the fact that the Kerry camp was offering no comment on the matter— perhaps for fear of earning a 'conspiracy buff' label for the candidate himself—may also have made reporters skittish. Jeffrey Klein, a founding editor of *Mother Jones* magazine, told *Mother Jones* (on-line edition, 10/30/04) he had called a number of contacts at leading news organizations across the country, and was told that unless the Kerry campaign raised the issue, they couldn't pursue it."

The bizarre calculus that says developments in an election campaign are not news unless a candidate decides to make them so has become deeply ingrained in American journalistic practice, particularly at the level of national politics. Television networks and newspapers have become increasingly averse to stepping out on limbs in pursuit of stories; they prefer to have a talking head from one major party or the other make an outrageous claim and report it, rather than actually commit acts of journalism. It's cheaper and safer—and "cheap" and "safe" are watchwords of media managers. But the mothership of American media, the *New York Times,* apparently chose to break ranks in October of 2004 and pursue the humpback president story. Unfortunately, the ensuing article, which reportedly revealed details of how Bush had worn the electronic device, did not appear as had been planned during the week before the election. As Lindorff revealed, "several sources, including a journalist at the *Times,* have told *Extra!* that the paper put a good deal of effort into this important story about presidential competence and integrity; they claim that a story was written, edited and scheduled to run on several different days, before senior editors finally axed it at the last minute on Wednesday evening, October 27. A *Times* journalist, who said that *Times* staffers were 'pretty upset' about the killing of the story, claims the senior editors felt Thursday was 'too close' to the election to run such a piece. E-mails from the *Times* to the NASA scientist (who was a key source) corroborate these sources' accounts."

Ben Bagdikian, the former *Washington Post* reporter and editor who went on to a distinguished career as dean of the University of California at Berkeley's School of Journalism, expressed proper outrage over reports that the *Times* had chosen to kill the story. "I cannot imagine a paper I worked for turning down a story like this before an election. This was credible photographic evidence not about breaking the rules, but of a total lack of integrity on the part of the president, evidence that he'd cheated in the debate, and also of a lack of confidence in his ability on the part of his campaign," said Bagdikian. "I'm shocked to hear top management decided not to run such a story." Unlike contemporary editors, Bagdikian, one of the great investigative reporters of the twentieth century, put the *Times'* decision in proper perspective: "Cheating on a debate should affect an election. The decision not to let people know this story could affect the history of the United States."

ORWELLIAN DETOURS

The final days of the campaign instead focused on another media diversion: the predictable pre-election tape from Osama bin Laden.

The al Qaeda leaders pre-election ruminations, which the television networks refused to air in their entirety, became the set piece for a final round of talking-head discussions about the president's war on terror. In a classic example of horse-race journalism trumping substance, many of the discussions revolved around the question of whether bin Laden's decision to surface himself at the last moment favored Bush, who had not caught the "most wanted man," or Kerry, who conservatives had painted as too soft to go after the terrorists. The smart money stated that refocusing the campaign in its final stages on the national security and defense issues that had favored the president from September 11, 2001, onward was beneficial to his re-election prospects.

If there is any uncertainty about how bin Laden played, however, there is no doubt about the way in which another media moment during the final stages of the 2004 campaign favored Bush in every sense and closed the campaign on an appropriately Orwellian note.

George Orwell—who observed that "political language . . . is designed to make lies sound truthful and murder respectable, and to give the appearance of solidity to pure wind"—anticipated a future in which a propagandistic media would produce a steady stream of up-is-down, right-is-wrong, war-is-peace lies in order to impose the will of a governing elite upon the subject citizenry. Orwell reckoned this ultimate diminution of democracy would come in 1984. Genius though he was, the author missed the mark by 20 years.

The controversy regarding the Sinclair Broadcast Group's scheme to air the truth-impaired mockumentary *Stolen Honor* less than two weeks before the election, in an attempt to stall any momentum that Kerry's campaign might have gained from the presidential debates, was the reality-TV version of *1984*.

Forget about *Stolen Honor: Wounds That Never Heal*. The comic attempt at a documentary was nothing more than a forty-two-minute Swift Boat Veterans for Truth–style television commercial produced by a former longtime employee of Tom Ridge, the boss of

Bush's Department of Homeland Security—an agency that paid daily homage to Orwell with everything from its name to the color-coded terrorism warnings it issued on a regular basis during the campaign.

But don't forget about the Sinclair Broadcast Group. Anyone who wanted to see the Orwellian media future that the Bush administration envisioned needed to pay close attention to Sinclair. The cobbled-together collection of television properties was not a network but a media-holding company that owned sixty-two of the most miserable excuses for broadcast outlets in the country.

"Quality" has never been a watchword for Sinclair, a firm that—with waivers, nods, and winks from industry allies at the Federal Communications Commission—pioneered the one-size-fits-all approach to mass media. Sinclair's model was simple: It bought TV stations in long-suffering communities, fired in-house staffers, and began feeding the locals a steady diet of disembodied and disengaged content spewed out of the company's media mill near Baltimore.

Sinclair went so far as to experiment with the so-called distance-casting of weather reports. Sinclair's stormbots read local forecasts for communities around the country while standing in front of ever-changing weather maps at the firm's suburban Baltimore bunker.

But the main product of Sinclair's media mill during the 2004 campaign was a spew of right-wing dogma drooled from the lips of Mark Hyman, the company's vice president for corporate relations. Ideologically in sync with the bosses at Sinclair—who contributed more than $170,000 to Republican causes from the mid-1990s on, including close to $60,000 in the 2004 campaign—Hyman force-fed editorials to all sixty-two company-owned stations in order to shore up the conservative cause. And a good deal of shoring up those editorials could do, as Sinclair's stations reach twenty-five percent of all American households.

Hyman made FOX's Sean Hannity sound like a sensible moderate. The Sinclair mouthpiece specialized in scorched-earth attacks on anyone who saw through the distortions of the Bush administration. Whenever mainstream media outlets practiced anything akin to jour-

nalism, Hyman condemned the offending outlets as the "hate America crowd." He referred to members of Congress who criticize the war in Iraq as "unpatriotic politicians who hate our military." When it came to the presidential contest, Hyman served as a one-man propaganda machine, spinning out anti-Kerry commentaries and repeating even the most discredited lies about Kerry's Vietnam record on stations that broadcast in at least eleven of the year's seventeen battleground states. If Hyman's goal was to make FOX look fair and balanced by comparison with Sinclair, he's succeeded.

When the controversy about Sinclair's decision to scrap regular programming in order to air *Stolen Honor* heated up, Hyman went spinning into Orwellian overdrive. He accused the nation's broadcast and cable networks—including, presumably, Rupert Murdoch's Republicans-*uber-alles* FOX network—of collaborating to suppress anti-Kerry news. Because they have not aired *Stolen Honor* or given enough time to the embittered Kerry critics featured in the production, Hyman said, "they are acting like Holocaust deniers."

Orwell would have had to stretch even his creative powers to come up with a propagandist who compared the decisions of news departments not to cover discredited claims with the denial of Nazi genocide. But Hyman didn't stop there. He updated his slurs to the immediate moment. When Democrats suggested that Sinclair's decision to air the anti-Kerry documentary so close to the election needed to be seen as an in-kind contribution to Bush and the Republicans, Hyman replied, "If you use that logic and reasoning, that means every car bomb in Iraq would be considered an in-kind contribution to John Kerry."

Hyman was, of course, wrong. But the Orwellian propagandist did not blink in the face of reality. He simply lied louder.

Issues of truth and falsehood had never been a particularly significant concern for the "Dear Mr. Fantasy" of the right. Hyman did not bother to abide even by the exceptionally low standards of accuracy that prevail among conservative commentators. Rather, he peddled partisan talking points that were written with an eye toward aiding Republicans and afflicting Democrats and he guided a company that did the same, by refusing to air even noncontroversial Democratic National Committee commercials, and, as we discussed in chapter 3, by censoring an ABC-TV *Nightline* broadcast that consisted of the names and photographs of Americans killed in Iraq.

Objections from media activists associated with Media Matters, Common Cause, Free Press, and a host of other groups, along with complaints from members of Congress and Sinclair's own Washington bureau chief, Jonathan Leiberman—who was fired after he said of the documentary, "Call it commentary, call it editorial, call it programming, but don't call it news"—forced the network to back off its initial plan to package the documentary into an evening of attacks on Kerry. But Hyman's incendiary appearances on most of the nation's major broadcast and cable news and commentary programs had succeeded in getting the bogus criticisms of Kerry's Vietnam record pushed back into the forefront of public consciousness just before the election. Thus, while Sinclair may have had to back off, the rest of the media, susceptible as ever to spin, had done the deed that Hyman and his colleagues had set out to accomplish.

Referring to Sinclair's approach to the 2004 race, FCC member Michael Copps, the commission's most consistent critic of big media's abuses, said, "This is an abuse of the public trust. And it is proof positive of media consolidation run amok when one owner can use the public airwaves to blanket the country with its political ideology—whether liberal or conservative."

Copps added that "some will undoubtedly question if this is appropriate stewardship of the public airwaves . . . It is a sad fact that the explicit public interest protections we once had to ensure balance continue to be weakened by the Federal Communications Commission while it allows media conglomerates to get even bigger. Sinclair, and the FCC, are taking us down a dangerous road."

The Sinclair episode also pointed to the sheer and utter corruption of the U.S. media system. Massive firms like Sinclair get lucrative monopoly licenses (for free) from the government to do broadcasting on the public airwaves. In fact, their entire business is predicated upon getting these valuable monopoly licenses at no charge; it is a million miles from a free market operation. The firm, Sinclair in this case, then aggressively pushes progovernment propaganda to help the government get reelected, thereby abusing the spirit and letter of the law. The duly reelected government then proceeds to eliminate media ownership rules so Sinclair can then gobble up more broadcasting licenses around the country and continue with its propaganda. A win-win situation for Sinclair and Bush; a complete travesty for public policy and for a free press.

If George Orwell had been around, he would have recognized that the road to 1984 had turned into the campaign trail of 2004.

On November 2, the trail ran out. Election Day itself was a mess, particularly in the critical battleground state of Ohio, which would give Bush the electoral votes he needed to claim the presidency. U.S. Representative John Conyers, the ranking Democrat on the House Judiciary Committee, explained in *Preserving Democracy: What Went Wrong in Ohio,* a remarkably detailed and well-reasoned report on ill-prepared poll workers, broken rules, failed equipment, missing ballots, and miscounted votes in the Buckeye State: "We have found numerous, serious irregularities in the Ohio presidential election, which resulted in a significant disenfranchisement of voters. Cumulatively, these irregularities, which affected hundreds of thousands of votes and voters in Ohio, raise grave doubts regarding whether it can be said that Ohio electors selected on December 13, 2004, were chosen in a manner that conforms to Ohio law, let alone federal requirements and constitutional standards."

The Ohio debacle never earned the national media attention that was accorded the Florida recount of presidential votes cast in the 2000 contest between Bush and former Vice President Al Gore. In part, this was Kerry's fault. Rather than holding to the standard that an election ought not be considered settled until serious concerns about disenfranchisement had been resolved, Kerry and his aides determined that it was unlikely that they would prevail in a standard recount and folded their campaign on the day after the election. At that point, most U.S. media, with the notable exceptions of MSNBC's Keith Obermann and a few others, checked out. A media that relies primarily on official sources and studiously avoids risk and expense was not going to launch an investigation into the question of whether citizens who tended to be poor and working-class, young and African-American had been disenfranchised. Only if they had the hook of a candidate refusing to concede would most mainstream journalists have paid attention to the Ohio controversy. And Kerry was headed for a European vacation. Grassroots activists, many of them associated with the Green and Libertarian parties, did get Conyers and a few other members of Congress to pay attention. They even succeeded in forcing a challenge to the counting of Ohio's electoral votes—when California Senator Barbara Boxer sided with members of the Congressional Black Caucus to object—but they could not get the media to treat them as anything more than the conspiracy buffs and sore losers that the Republicans portrayed them as.

So the 2004 campaign ended on the note where it began, the note that Karl Rove and the Bush team had wisely counted on. American media, so easily spun, so frightened of criticism, so worried about the bottom line, so understaffed, so lazy, so unquestioning, so dysfunctional, had played precisely the role that those in power would ask of it. The established order was reinforced. And democracy was kept in check for another four years.

MAYBE IT'S THE PAPERS THEY'RE READING

The best postmortems came, as they so frequently have in recent years, from abroad. Indeed, the most pointed question asked in the aftermath of the 2004 U.S. election came from a British newspaper, the *Daily Mirror,* which inquired over a picture of George W. Bush, "How can 59,054,087 people be so dumb?"

A few days later, another British newspaper answered the question. A marketing campaign seeking international subscribers for the *Weekly Guardian,* one of the most respected publications in the world, featured images of a dancing Bush and noted that, "Many US citizens think the world backed the war in Iraq. Maybe it's the papers they're reading."

The weekly compendium of articles and analyses of global affairs from Britain's *Guardian* newspaper has long been regarded as an antidote to government-controlled, -spun, and inept local media. Nelson Mandela, when he was held in South Africa's Pollsmor Prison, referred to the *Weekly Guardian* as a "window on the wider world."

But is it really appropriate to compare the United States in 2004 with a warped media market like South Africa during apartheid days?

Actually, the comparison may be a bit unfair to South African media in the apartheid era, when many courageous journalists struggled to speak truth to power.

No serious observer of the current circumstances in the United States would suggest that our major media serves the cause of democracy. Years of consolidation and bottom-line pressures have forced even once-responsible newspapers and broadcast networks to allow entertainment and commercial values to supersede civic and democratic values when making news decisions. And the determination to color within the lines of official spin is such that even the supposed pinnacles of the profession—the *New York Times,* the *Washington Post,* and CBS News' *60 Minutes*—have been forced to acknowledge that they got the story of the rush to war with Iraq wrong.

There can be apologies. But there cannot be excuses because, of course, media in the rest of the world got that story right.

Getting the story wrong matters. There are consequences when major media blow it. As the *Weekly Guardian*'s marketing campaign suggested, a lot of Americans voted for George W. Bush on November 2, 2004, on the basis of wrong assumptions.

According to a survey conducted during the fall campaign season by the Program on International Policy Attitudes (PIPA)—a joint initiative of the Center on Policy Attitudes and the Center for International and Security Studies at the University of Maryland School of Public Affairs—a lot of what Americans know is wrong.

Despite the fact that surveys by the Gallup organization and other polling firms have repeatedly confirmed that the vast majority of citizens of other countries opposed the war in Iraq, the PIPA survey found that only 31 percent of Bush supporters recognized that the majority of people in the world opposed the Bush administration's decision to invade Iraq.

Amazingly, according to the PIPA poll, 57 percent of Bush supporters assumed that the majority of people in the world would favor Bush's reelection, while 33 percent assumed that global views regarding Bush were evenly divided. Only 9 percent of Bush backers correctly assumed that Kerry was the world's choice.

That wasn't the end of the misperception.

"Even after the final report of Charles Duelfer to Congress saying that Iraq did not have a significant WMD program, 72 percent of Bush supporters continue to believe that Iraq had actual WMD (47 percent) or a major program for developing them (25 percent)," explained the summary of PIPA's polling. "Fifty-six percent assume that most experts believe Iraq had actual WMD and 57 percent also assume, incorrectly, that Duelfer concluded Iraq had at least a major WMD program."

"Similarly," the pollsters found, "75 percent of Bush supporters continue to believe that Iraq was providing substantial support to al Qaeda, and 63 percent believe that clear evidence of this support has been found. Sixty percent of Bush supporters assume that this is also the conclusion of most experts, and 55 percent assume, incorrectly, that this was the conclusion of the 9/11 Commission."

PIPA analysts suggested that the "tendency of Bush supporters to ignore dissonant information" formed part of the explanation for these numbers. And there is something to that. After all, Kerry backers displayed a far sounder sense of reality in PIPA surveys. But unless we want to assume that close to 60 million Americans look at the world only through Bush-colored glasses, there has to be some acceptance of the fact that good citizens who consume American media come away with dramatic misconceptions about the most vital issues of the day.

Sure, FOX warps facts intentionally. But what about CBS, NBC, ABC, CNN, *USA Today,* the *New York Times,* and the *Washington Post,* as well as most local media across the country? They may strive to be more accurate than FOX or talk-radio personalities such as Rush Limbaugh. But they still fed the American people an inaccurate picture when they allowed the Bush team to peddle lies about Iraq and other issues without aggressively and consistently challenging those misstatements of fact.

America has many great journalists. And there are still good newspapers, magazines, and broadcast programs. But, taken as a whole, U.S. media—with its obsessive focus on John Kerry's Vietnam record, its neglect of fundamental economic and environmental issues, and its stenographic repetition of even the most absurd claims by the president and vice president—warped the debate in 2004.

Some of those 59,054,087 Bush voters may have been dumb.

But a far better explanation for the election result came in the *Weekly Guardian*'s observation that the explanation for what ails American democracy has less to do with parties and candidates than it does with the media Americans have been consuming.

CHAPTER 6

MEDIA FOR A PEOPLE WHO MEAN TO BE THEIR OWN GOVERNORS

"A free press is not a privilege but an organic necessity in a great society."

—Walter Lippmann

It is not difficult to fill a book with complaints about contemporary media. But complaints are only of value if they come in the context of a call to address them. The point of detailing the damage done to democracy by a media system that cannot be trusted to cover wars and elections is to get citizens mad enough to demand the changes that will allow a more responsible and democracy-sustaining media to develop.

We believe, as Walter Lippmann did, that a free, diverse, and courageous media are essential not merely to the perpetuation of democratic institutions but to the creation and preservation of a great society. Necessarily, we also believe that the absence of such media undermine not merely democracy but the progress toward the more just, humane, and prosperous country that America can be.

It is that faith that feeds our deep concern regarding the crisis of the media in the United States, a crisis that threatens the existence of viable self-government as well as the potential for genuine progress. The political culture that accompanies the media crisis is not abstract; it is typified by political demoralization, growing social and economic inequality, militarism and irrationalism, and rampant, even routinized, corruption. It is a long-term crisis, determined by complex factors, but in the end rooted in corrupt media policymaking that has allowed the media system to become primarily a means of expanding the profits of a relatively small number of massive firms, rather than providing the oxygen of democracy.

The crisis manifests itself in innumerable ways, but in this book we have concentrated upon what are arguably the two most important duties of a free press: how it engages the citizenry to permit them to monitor the war-making power of the government; and how it provides the necessary information such that citizens can participate meaningfully in elections. If the media system fails in these areas, whatever good it does otherwise is of limited value. Under the auspices of our mainstream media, we invaded a nation on bogus grounds, and have arguably left the world a much more dangerous place. We held a money-drenched presidential election that managed to avoid large issues facing our country and world. Much as Madison feared, our polity is increasingly a tragedy and a farce. But there is nothing funny about it.

MEDIA REFORM RETURNS TO THE POLITICAL STAGE

Concerns about the nature of U.S. democracy are not new, nor is criticism of the media. For generations, though, the unstated presupposition of political discourse was that the media system was for better or for worse entrenched and unchangeable. The belief was that if social movements organized to change the political culture of the country—e.g., the labor, civil rights, and feminist movements from the 1930s into the 1970s or the conservative movements since the 1980s—their successes would be reflected in more generous and favorable treatment by the media system. The media were to be regarded as a dependent variable.

But in recent years, a new understanding has developed that the media system itself must be changed, that the problems of the media cannot be separated from the political arena. As we have demonstrated, the media system is a significant factor in how power operates in the United States, and it is a factor that if left unexamined and unchallenged, reduces the capacity of citizens to constructively engage in public life. To make this journey from accepting the media status quo as inevitable to something we can and must change, we must demolish the one huge myth that has protected entrenched media power from the reckoning it so richly deserves: the notion that our media system is a free market system, a system ordained by the Founding Fathers (if not an even higher force), and protected from public intervention by the First Amendment to the Constitution.

For starters, our media system is not a free market system. Sure, firms compete to maximize profits, but that does not a free market make. The handful of firms that largely determine America's media diet are all the recipients of massive government privileges, monopoly franchises, and subsidies. While government plays an important role in creating markets generally, it plays an even greater role in the realm of media. What are these monopoly franchises and subsidies? Consider the government granting and enforcement (at little or no charge) of monopoly rights to radio and TV channels and the cable and satellite TV systems. Or consider copyright, which is nothing but an artificial government creation to protect monopoly and prevent competition. The value of these subsidies and monopoly licenses alone has never been formally calculated, but by all accounts runs into the tens or hundreds of billions of dollars on an annual basis.

Don't get us wrong. We are not opposed to such subsidies per se. In fact, we think there is a necessary role for enlightened public subsidies and policies to encourage a truly free press. There is no default media system that would result if the government simply removed itself. Any media system—free market or whatever—requires extensive government policymaking.

That is why the term "deregulation" is so misleading and propagandistic when applied to media policy debates. We are often told, for example, that radio broadcasting was deregulated in 1996, when the Telecommunications Act removed any limit on the number of monopoly radio licenses a single firm could possess. As a result a company like Clear Channel, which for generations had been limited to owning less than a dozen stations nationally, could gobble up over 1,200 radio stations within a few years. The consequences for radio broadcasting of this concentrated ownership have been disastrous, with localism declining while commercialism is ratcheted upwards. Is this deregulation? Try to broadcast on one of the frequencies Clear Channel is presently using, saying that since radio is now deregulated, it is your turn to use the airwaves. If you persist, you will do twenty years in Leavenworth or some other federal abode.

In fact, radio is as regulated today as it has ever been, only it is regulated to serve the interest of corporations like Clear Channel. Whenever you see the term "deregulation," substitute the following more accurate term: "reregulation serving powerful corporate interests with no pretense of serving the public." The fact is that regulation is unavoidable; the question is how that regulation will be deployed and in whose interests.

This is where the central role of media policy debates enters the picture. It is these debates that will determine the values and policies that guide what type of media system we have in the United States. And it is here that we see the crisis of the American media in full bloom. For many decades the core policies that have created the U.S. media system have been made quietly behind closed doors in deliberations dominated by powerful commercial interests. The public has known nothing of these policy discussions and is besieged by a phalanx of PR agents informing us that this is a natural free-market media system that gives the people what they want. The stench of corruption is palpable.

This leads to the other half of the myth that protects entrenched corporate media power: the notion that the media status quo is the one ordained by the Founding Fathers; that the First Amendment's provision for freedom of the press is meant to protect the commercial interests of media owners from any government interference; that freedom of the press, as A. J. Liebling famously put it, "belongs to those who own one." This part of the myth is nothing short of preposterous.

The founders, most notably Madison and Jefferson, understood clearly the need for policies and subsidies to spawn a viable free press; they had no illusions that simply turning the press system over to commercial interests to maximize profit would be satisfactory. Freedom of the press meant the right of all citizens to have a rich and diverse press system, not the right of owners to do whatever they wished to maximize profit without concern for the public. As a result of debates that sometimes generated considerable public attention, massive printing and postal subsidies established perhaps the most vibrant print culture in the world in the first half of the nineteenth-century, and helped make the northern United States, for all its flaws, arguably the most egalitarian and democratic nation in the world. These were either content-neutral subsidies, meaning they did not favor a specific point of view, or they were balanced subsidies that benefited more than one political party or faction.

As dramatic new media technologies emerged, such as the telegraph, telephone, and radio, they spawned considerable public debates about how they could best be deployed. It was not assumed ipso facto that media and communication should be turned over to commercial interests. When concentration of newspaper ownership generated a massive crisis in journalism—featuring rampant sensationalism along with blatant antilabor partisanship—it prompted a level of public criticism rarely equaled. This led to the rise of professional journalism, as we discussed in chapter 2.

Over the course of the twentieth century as media industries have become bigger and more profitable, the policymaking process has become increasingly corrupt, and further removed from public awareness, not to mention participation. When television was launched in the 1940s, the lucrative channels were basically given to the major radio networks and their affiliates to be supported by advertising, and there was not a shred of public discussion. Few Americans were aware that debating the structure of television was even an option. Setting an all-too-familiar pattern, the Federal Communications Commission chairman responsible for the TV plan left the government shortly afterward to become an executive at NBC. There are often tremendous fights among media corporations and media industries over who should get which benefits of government regulations, subsidies, and policies, which is why their lobbies are so enormous: to do battle with each other. But these firms all agree that it is their system and the public has no claim to it.

Understood this way, that corrupt policymaking is responsible for a media system that fails to serve the public effectively, the solution to the crisis becomes evident. What is necessary is to generate widespread popular involvement in media policymaking debates. This is the core principle that guides the formation of a democratic media. The more informed public participation in media policymaking, the greater the likelihood that the resulting system will serve the broad public. It is Democracy 101.

For many years, even when the analyses of the media situation in the United States came to the conclusion that democratizing reforms were needed, actual public participation was considered all but impossible. The corporate media lobby was too powerful. The giant media firms owned the politicians and controlled how the public would learn about the issue. As important as media were in the abstract, this was not a pressing issue to most people, who were portrayed as being content with the status quo, if not elated about it. To most observers, even those most sympathetic to the need to reform the media system, the prospects for establishing a widespread media reform movement seemed about as good as the prospects for a mass movement to protest the existence of the Rocky Mountains.

But over the past two decades a media reform movement has come into being in the United States. Driven by concerns ranging from lousy journalism and hypercommercialism to racist and sexist content and declining localism, movements for media reform first grew on the margins of society, beneath the corporate media radar. In this manner, media reform had its own prehistory, much like the civil rights, feminist, and environmental movements. People concerned with issues of social justice or war and peace increasingly recognized that the existing media system was a profound barrier to progress, and, at times, a powerful force for reaction. In retrospect, the only question is why it took this movement so long to take off.

The contemporary media reform movement exploded into public consciousness in 2003, with the campaign to oppose the FCC's efforts to relax or eliminate media ownership rules that prevented firms from gobbling up all the government-granted monopoly broadcast licenses and then using profits from those government franchises to swallow all the other media in a community or the nation. In January 2003, only a few thousand Americans were even aware of the FCC proceedings. By the end of the year, nearly three million people from across the political spectrum had registered their opposition to media concentration with both the FCC and Congress. When a federal court eventually threw out the FCC's relaxed media ownership rules in 2004, it cited this public opposition in its ruling.

This volcanic eruption was entirely unexpected by just about everyone. What was especially bizarre was the extent to which people became concerned with what seems like technical or relatively marginal changes in ownership rules. The explanation is simple: For the first time millions of Americans saw the truth about media in the United States, that the media system is not natural but based upon policies that have been made in their name but without their informed consent. It is not just a right, but a duty, for a free people to establish a free press. Years of personal frustrations with media found an avenue for protest, activism, and reform.

We are still in the early stages of this process, so it is impossible to assess how profound this change has been; two decades from now it may look like the Montgomery bus boycott or it could be a mere blip on the historical screen. But there is little doubt that media has become a political issue in the United States as it has not been since the Progressive Era. One telling indicator is that due to membership pressure, the large public interest group Common Cause has made media reform one of its core issues, after having nothing to do with the issue for three decades. A more striking indicator was polling conducted by

MoveOn.org and True Majority of their millions of members in late 2004 and early 2005, asking what they considered the most important issues to work on for the coming years. In each poll, media reform ranked second, ahead of peace, health care, education, and social justice. We think it is safe to say that in a similar poll conducted five years earlier, media reform would not have ranked in the top ten; a similar poll fifteen or twenty years ago probably would not have even countenanced media reform as a category.

The times they are a–changin'.

THREE BRANCHES OF THE MEDIA REFORM MOVEMENT

The media reform movement has three main components. All three have long histories, and the three are integrally connected; in the final analysis they rise and fall together. (There is a degree competition for scarce funding by actors in each of the three sectors of the media reform movement, and this can feed a divisiveness that can be counterproductive.) Unless this interdependence is grasped and accepted by the movement as a whole, the political prospects for any of the three branches as well as the media reform movement writ large will be reduced markedly. The three areas are: 1) media criticism/education/ literacy; 2) producing independent media; and 3) political organizing for structural media reform, aka media policy activism. (In fact, there is a fourth area, which is promoting powerful democratic trade unions for media workers, so as to provide a balance to corporate media power within the existing system, and to conceivably participate in efforts to restructure the media system. But that aspect of the movement at present is subsumed in the other three areas, especially number three.)

There is a long and rich tradition of media criticism in the United States, particularly directed at journalism. It blossomed during the Progressive Era and was kept alive through the twentieth century by the likes of Upton Sinclair, George Seldes, A. J. Liebling, and the journalism reviews that sprouted in the 1960s. By the 1980s, figures ranging from Ben Bagdikian, Noam Chomsky, and Edward S. Herman to Alexander Cockburn and Gloria Steinem brought increased prominence to media activism, and made it a staple component of political activism. By the late 1980s, Fairness & Accuracy In Reporting (FAIR) had been founded. This group highlighted the ways in which mainstream journalism reinforced the political values and interests of those atop the socio-economic structure in the United States.

This work has been very useful because it alerts citizens to be more skeptical of what they read, see, and hear in the news media, and it serves as an important watchdog over the press to keep the news media aware of flawed coverage. Media criticism can be instrumental in making the commercial status quo operate in the public interest as much as possible. But there are limits to what jawboning the dominant commercial media with stellar criticism can produce. The best of this criticism points toward the conclusion that the problems with journalism are hard-wired into the system, and the only way to solve the problems in a satisfactory manner is through structural change. Unless the criticism is tied to political organizing in order to change the system, it can only go so far. There is a risk that media critics will settle into a niche on the margins, delighting some and being dismissed as ineffectual bellyachers by others.

In short, media criticism needs the other branches of the media reform movement—both independent media that respond to and address this criticism as well as policy activism to feed off the criticism to change the system—to grow and remain viable. And in the context of such a movement, the need for media criticism increases. As a result, in the past few years media criticism has grown dramatically. From numerous weblogs and columns by veteran media watchers like Danny Schechter, Bob Somerby, Jenn Pozner, and Norman Solomon and the expanded operations of FAIR to the new group Media Matters for America and the superb work of the Center for Media and Democracy in Madison, Wisconsin, and the Media Education Foundation in Northampton, Massachusetts—to mention but a few examples—media criticism has become a staple of the political and intellectual landscape, and of the media reform movement.

It is important to note that media criticism is not restricted to journalism. Much of the movement has been fueled by concerns with entertainment programming. For decades there has been a movement in the United States and worldwide to establish "media literacy" as a core part of the K–12 curriculum in our schools. The basic idea is that as audio-visual media have replaced print as the dominant technology, we need a literacy in film, TV, and digital media commensurate with our current education in reading and writing. Media literacy makes students aware of how media systems work, what the strategies of media producers are, and how students can avoid being manipulated by media. At its best, media literacy makes students see themselves as citizens in a media world, rather than consumers of whatever advertisers and media firms place before them. But media literacy doesn't fall from the sky and land in the classroom. It only exists as a result of local community organizing to get it placed in school curricula. It exists as a result of policy struggles.

Producing independent or alternative media is hardly a new phenomenon either. It has been a staple of U.S. history from the beginning; one can barely conceive of the abolitionists, suffragists, or labor movement without their own media. One of the recurring criticisms of the U.S. commercial media system has been the manner in which it has made it ever more difficult for individuals to successfully launch new commercially viable media. Today, the emergence of the Internet and the broader digital communication revolution has radically lowered production costs and reduced distribution costs to, at times, almost nothing. These changes have democratized media production and consumption. In this context we are experiencing an unprecedented boom in independent media. The media system is being radically reconstructed at a technological level; how much that plays out at an institutional level, and what the implications are for altering journalism is a topic of much speculation. Dan Gillmor, for instance, makes an exciting and provocative case for the use of new technologies to provide the basis for a revolutionary expansion of citizens' journalism and democracy.

More than a few people have become so taken with the Internet and the blogosphere that they claim the old media are increasingly irrelevant and can now be ignored. We can all work on our websites and blogs and enter into chats with others who share our interests. The big media firms are like dinosaurs soon to become extinct. This critique ranges from promarket libertarians, and, as we discuss below, corporate media bosses, to folks on the political Left ranging from some folks associated with the independent media center movement to Alexander Cockburn, co-editor of the CounterPunch website. Cockburn advised readers of his *Nation* column to stop whining about the media because the corporate system is dying, and to focus all attention on doing material on the Internet, which is a level playing field and the future of all media. "[W]e have the web," Cockburn states. "We're infinitely better off than we were thirty years ago."

It is hard not to be dazzled by what is taking place with the Internet, and by what changes are looming on the visible horizon. Hugh Hewitt tells us the blogosphere is "smashing the old media monopoly and giving individuals power in the marketplace of ideas." But in our view it would be a mistake, a fatal mistake, to assume these new technologies obviate any concern for media policy matters, or for criticism of the existing commercial media system. These technologies will not allow us to leapfrog the hard world of media politics; in fact, it is government policy decisions that will largely determine how these technologies develop. In other words, these technologies *increase* the importance of media policy fights exponentially.

Why is this?

For starters, the notion that the new world of digital media is going to obliterate conventional media is exaggerated. It is true that some traditional media like newspapers, radio, and over-the-air television are seeing their usage numbers stagnate or decline. But that does not mean these conglomerates are going out of business. The old media have held out fairly well, and power in the traditional media marketplace has translated into power in the digital media marketplace. It is worth noting that in the dozen or so years since the advent of the World Wide Web and the commercialized Internet, very few commercially viable online media content providers have been launched. (Salon.com is a rare success story, but it is tiny next to the Disneys and Time Warners.) Research continually demonstrates that the most visited news and information websites are owned by the largest media conglomerates. The technology has not proved sufficient to break up the market power of the giants. Indeed, this market power is allowing for convergence, for a digital media system to emerge where the traditional media giants remain dominant.

It is also worth noting that the media giants will don nose rings, sport tattoos, wear green-hair Mohawk wigs and gladly promote the idea that the hip new technologies are rendering them ineffectual; therefore, they argue, there is no need for media ownership rules. The giants want to be able to gobble up all the old media they can, which would make it that much more difficult for the Internet to provide an alternative. Moreover, as the giants get bigger, it increases their ability to dictate policy behind closed doors in Washington.

Moreover, all blogs are not created equal. Much has been made about how blogs and websites have played such a crucial role in, say, derailing an attempt by Dan Rather and CBS News in September to cover George W. Bush's military record. What was most striking about this was less the power of citizen journalists armed with blogs than the power of blogs closely linked to the Republican party and right-wing political operatives. Once these blogs ran with the story, it benefited from the echo chamber effect on FOX News and talk radio and soon was foisted into the news agenda of all media. The blogosphere abounds with superb critical analysis of all sorts of foibles of the Bush administration that are of vastly greater importance than the Rather/CBS News incident, but they hardly ever see the light of day. Without a broader sense of media strategy, blogs can only have so much influence over the media system and the political system.

Lost in the excitement of new technologies is the reality that labor and resources are necessary to create good media. Merely having a blog or a website does not insure the solid work needed to keep an audience over the long haul. Even including the large number of blogs and websites, evidence suggests there are actually fewer full-time working reporters covering news today than there were a decade ago. The market, as we note in chapter 2, has declared war on journalism, and the technology will not regenerate it magically. The historical record has made it clear that relying upon volunteer labor and donations cannot be sufficient to sustain a viable media system. The historical record has also demonstrated that a media system dominated by commercial institutions supported by advertising puts real limits on media. That is why much of the independent media exists.

There is an unavoidable issue of how to provide material support for media content, and this is an issue that has existed since the dawn of media. Postal subsidies, for example, were important to the survival of the abolitionist press in the nineteenth century. The importance of subsidies only increases in the digital era. At present the federal government provides billions of dollars worth of subsidies to commercial media on an annual basis, as noted above. Should the people of this country simply concede these corrupt subsidies and make do with zilch as they pursue their blogs, or should they fight to see that subsidies suit the public interest, or, if they so desire, should they see them eliminated? These are all legitimate questions in an unavoidable policy fight.

Effective democratic journalism not only requires material support, it requires institutional support. If journalism is doing what it must do, at some point it will invariably earn the wrath of those in power, be it in government or the private sector. Media institutions are necessary to protect journalists and promote their ability to do good work. For the most pressing example of the need for viable media institutions today, consider the current administration's obsession with increasing government secrecy. If much of what governments and powerful corporations do is legally and/or effectively off-limits to public inspection or review, all the blogs in the world might not amount to a hill of beans. One of the core functions of media institutions is to press for openness of records, to protect and preserve democratic liberties and citizen control over the polity. It is the abject failure of our media conglomerates in this regard, their continual accommodation to the needs of those in power, which contributes to the case that their dominance of the media system is counterproductive to self-government.

Proponents of the "technology will set us free" school tend also to take for granted that the right to put up a website or have access to any website is built into the technology, when, in fact, it is a result of policies such as the common carrier provision in telecommunications law. The huge cable and phone companies—the main broadband providers at present—want to be able to discriminate and give preferential treatment to websites and users, because that is the path to ever greater riches. When the U.S. Supreme Court ruled in the *National Cable & Telecommunications Association v. Brand X Internet Services* case in June 2005 that cable companies did not necessarily have to honor the "common carrier" regulation that required telephone companies to open their wires to any prospective Internet Service Provider at a nondiscriminatory price, it threw down the gauntlet for a donnybrook of a policy fight at the FCC and in Congress over the next two years. If the telephone companies and cable companies are able to shirk the common carrier requirement, it could take the Internet very far away from being a universal public service.

Likewise, draconian copyright measures like those found in the Digital Millennium Copyright Act erect legal barbed wire all over cyberspace, and make it more difficult for people to successfully navigate and produce independent content. An entire range of crucial policy issues will determine the shape of our media system in the next few years, and unless there is widespread public participation, there is every reason to believe the digital system we get will be considerably less democratic than the technology allows.

We say this not to undermine the importance of independent media, but rather to put them into context. Doing independent media is central to the media reform movement. On the one hand, independent media can break stories and pioneer content that the dominant commercial system avoids. The independent media sector can force the dominant commercial sector to change its content accordingly or expose their irrelevance. It works hand-in-hand with media criticism in this manner.

On the other hand, independent media make the vision of the media reform movement concrete, showing in many cases what we are fighting for. Independent media often provide an information lifeline in periods of intense propaganda, such as the invasion and occupation of Iraq. And, of no small importance, independent media tend to be the only media that cover in any consequential way the activities of the media reform movement. Moreover, the media–reform movement is all about having people see themselves as active participants in media, not simply passive consumers. It is worth noting that a 2004 survey sponsored by the Knight Foundation found a sharp drop-off of support for freedom of the press and free speech among high school students. The reason? Among other factors according to the Knight researchers, policies that cut back funding for student media meant that fewer young people have an appreciation of what it means to do journalism and the importance of media institutions. Again, all roads lead back to policy.

Media policy reform is the third wing of the media reform movement. On the one hand, it is very simple. The unifying purpose of the movement is to see that there is widespread informed public participation on the policy issues upon which our media system is built. At this level, it is clearly a non-partisan issue, to be supported by all but those who benefit from the corrupt and secretive nature of media policymaking that has been the rule. And as a democratic movement, media reformers are committed to living with whatever policies emerge from a fair and open debate, though they may keep fighting on for reforms.

On the other hand, media policy is maddeningly complex. There are dozens of distinct media policy issues, and they are established at the local, state, national, and global level. There is no one button to push to solve all problems, and multiple policy reforms are necessary to have full effect upon the media system. If there are two central values that drive much of the U.S. media reform movement as it engages in these debates, they are the following: 1) to the extent the media system is commercial, it should be as competitive as possible; and, to the extent technology and economics permit, there should be a priority given to locally owned and operated media. In short, policies should attempt to make it easier for people to start their own commercial outlet; and 2) a purely commercial media system has distinct limitations, generating what economists call negative externalities. Therefore, it is imperative to establish a vibrant and heterogeneous nonprofit and noncommercial media sector.

CONTOURS OF MEDIA POLICY REFORM

As the media-reform movement has grown dramatically in the past few years, a handful of key areas are beginning to receive increased and sustained attention. Groups have emerged that work on specific issues, sometimes at the local level. In every area there are short-term struggles, sometimes defensive in nature, and long-run campaigns to seek structural change and substantively improve matters. There are six core areas that encompass much of the policy work in the media-reform movement.

First, there are policies to promote accountable, transparent policymaking, and viable self-government. On the one hand, this means removing the corruption in media policymaking, among politicians, in Congress, at the FCC, and across the country. It means having public hearings for core media policy decisions and it means developing legitimate mechanisms to generate public input on broadcast license renewals, cable TV franchise renewals, and Internet governance.

On the other hand, this means having the media do a better job of promoting fair and legitimate elections. As we have discussed, the media system is doing a dreadful job of covering candidates and elections in the United States. A significant factor is that many of the largest media firms receive massive revenues in every election cycle to carry political ads on TV that are often of dubious accuracy. In 2004, candidates, parties, and independent groups paid some $1.6 billion to TV stations to run political ads; the amount spent was more than double the amount spent in 2000, and four times the amount spent in 1996. This is clearly a growth industry, and political advertising has all but colonized political discourse in the United States. The money for these ads tends to come from wealthy Americans. There is little incentive for media to do serious election coverage in such a context. The huge election revenue also explains why the media conglomerates are to campaign finance reform what the National Rifle Association is to gun control. Campaign finance reform is a first cousin to media reform, and any route to success in the realm of campaign finance, or in making our elections work, must include changes in media policy.

Second, there are the numerous battles around media ownership policies. As numerous scholars have chronicled, the United States has undergone a striking wave of media consolidation in the past two decades, such that a handful of conglomerates rule the media kingdom. In the near term, this means organizing around the FCC's review of media ownership rules, specifically the number of government-granted monopoly licenses a single firm may possess, and what other outlets that firms possessing government monopoly licenses are permitted to acquire. This presently is a central organizing issue for the media reform movement, as the Bush administration has made the elimination or relaxation of these rules a high priority. If the administration succeeds, it will make the largest media firms grow much larger, and it will all but end what remains of independent local media ownership in the United States.

Looking down the road, the United States still has to reconcile its antitrust law with the degree of concentration in the media industry. Political corruption has heretofore made that impossible. At some point the question must be asked: What, on balance, are the costs and benefits of allowing massive conglomerates to dominate numerous media sectors? More broadly, it is clear that we need a coherent discussion concerning media ownership that factors in the emerging digital world. The media giants and their ideologues tell us that the rise of the Internet means there is no need for such a discussion and that they should be allowed to own whatever they want, since dissatisfied people can start their own blogs and bellyache to their heart's content. We disagree. We believe this is precisely the time for such a discussion, with the goal of generating a proactive policy.

Related to both the areas of democratic governance and ownership are policies concerning trade unions and media workers. Labor laws must protect the right of workers to organize unions without being subjected to harassment. Unions provide a necessary counterbalance to concentrated corporate media power and afford protection to whistle-blowers. And with unions taking the lead, we need policy debates about other forms of media institutions in addition to the existing commercial model, such as worker-run outlets and nonprofit cooperatives. In 2004, Carl Sessions Stepp wrote an important piece in the *American Journalism Review* suggesting nonprofit media may be far more conducive to promoting and protecting quality journalism. If that is the case, we need to start discussing its implications for media policymaking.

The third area for media reform activism concerns regulation and governance of the Internet. It is ironic that the Internet is sometimes held up as the creation of private enterprise, when in fact it is a testament to public sector investment and policymaking. It was built largely with federal taxpayer funds. How the Internet develops is going to be determined by a number of core policies in the United States and globally. What is clear is that the Internet poses a challenge to the business practices of the firms that currently dominate the media landscape, and that the outcome will be determined in the policy arena as much as or more than in the marketplace or in a research laboratory.

Consider broadband Internet service provision. Currently the field is dominated by enormous telephone and cable companies, all of which are built on government granted monopolies. They charge high prices for mediocre service and depend upon their semi-monopolistic power for their business model. New mesh wireless technology makes it possible to provide a less expensive and higher quality service as a public utility to the entire community, seriously reducing the digital (racial/class) divide. The cable and telephone giants are working incessantly to make it illegal for local communities to establish community Internet systems, to kill this child in the crib so to speak, and to see that standards and spectrum policies developed by the FCC also make this impossible. If they win, we can be assured that down the road their history books will tell us that Comcast and Verizon built the Internet and that they were its inevitable stewards in a free market economy. But the truth is that their grip on the future is based upon corrupt policymaking. Whenever the American people learn about the potential of community wireless Internet access, they are outraged at what the giants are doing to thwart it.

An important policy fight, one related to media ownership, involves copyright law. Copyright exists due to the nature of media economics where it is expensive to make the first copy of something but relatively inexpensive to make subsequent copies. Copyright gives producers monopoly rights to their content for a given period of time so they can make sufficient income from it in order to have incentive to continue to produce new content. At this level, we think copyright is a necessary and useful policy, and we need to see that creators have protection along these lines in the future. But copyright is, in effect, a sanctioned monopoly and a public subsidy, because it countenances less competition and higher prices. Over the years, due purely to corrupt policymaking, copyright has been detached from its original intent and has become a property right for media corporations. By granting virtually permanent monopoly rights to media content—in contrast to the original term of fourteen years—copyright law has become a serious force in preventing competition and innovation in media markets.

With the rise of the Internet, copyright law becomes of paramount importance. The cost of distribution of content is virtually nothing on-line, providing a potential nightmare for commercial media content producers. The immediate response by the big guys has been to make copyright law ever more stringent, and attempt to undermine the logic, and genius, of the Internet. This is extraordinarily irrational from a social perspective. The desired course should be a genuine debate about how best to restructure media industries in view of the emergence of the Internet to assure that producers can support themselves, but also to see that ideas are as accessible as possible. Again, this is a complex policy issue that demands widespread public involvement if it is to begin to address concerns beyond those of wealthy media corporations.

The fourth area for media reform activism concerns subsidies and institutional structure to support nonprofit and noncommercial media. Even the best commercial media system—and we are light years away from that right now—will have limitations, so it is imperative that there be strong noncommercial media. This is a much broader demand than simply supporting and restructuring public radio and television, though those are important goals and of utmost importance in the immediate future. It also includes working to see that cable TV systems provide ample slots for local public access and for nonprofit and noncommercial channels. But this also gets to a central long-term issue for media reform activism. All the weblogs and websites in the world may only amount to a hill of beans if there are not the resources and institutional structures in place to generate quality content. Relying upon advertising or subscription fees or philanthropy alone is clearly insufficient and unsatisfactory.

What we need is to launch a serious discussion of ways we can foster a rich and diverse independent nonprofit and noncommercial media sector. One proposal, for example, by economist Dean Baker, would allow any American to deduct $100 from his or her federal income taxes and give it instead to any tax-exempt nonprofit outlet that meets existing IRS standards. This would provide a massive public subsidy, but it would not favor a particular point of view and would be independent of political control. Baker's condition for receiving the grant is that anything produced with the money would not be protected by copyright, but would instead go into the public domain. It would therefore be best suited toward journalism, which has less commercial value after its initial consumption, than toward other forms of content. We mention Baker's proposal not because it is necessarily the one we should adopt, but rather because it is a visionary way to begin thinking about methods to reorganize the media system to take advantage of emerging technologies and to promote democratic values. It is a discussion we desperately need to have in this nation.

The fifth area for media reform activism concerns hypercommercialism, or the incessant push of marketing into every nook and cranny of the media and our lives. Ironically the emergence of new technologies has not liberated us from commercialism as much as it has made advertising even more aggressive and ubiquitous. In short, the traditional boundary between the editorial/creative side and the commercial side of media is crumbling under commercial pressure. This is clearly a circumstance where the Internet will not set us free. The crisis of hypercommercialism affects journalism and is nothing short of a disaster with regard to our children, whose brains are being marinated in a commercial cocktail unlike any other generation of children has experienced before. In the short term, policy activism must work to limit the role and influence of advertising and marketers over media—and in other institutions like our schools—and eliminate surreptitious involvement in editorial/creative content. In the long term, we desperately need a debate and discussion about the appropriate role for advertising in our media and in our culture. This is a crisis that will only get worse until there is informed public debate.

The sixth and final area of media reform activism concerns global media policy. In this book we have discussed media policy issues as if they are primarily national and local in scope, as if they are totally unique to the United States. This is misleading. In fact all of the issues mentioned above are being fought out in every nation of the world, and each of these issues is strongly affected, if not determined, by policies generated by global organizations such as the World Trade Organization, the International Telecommunications Union, the World Intellectual Property Organization, and the United Nations, to name a few. In some cases the policies and treaties generated by these bodies override national law and regulation. Traditionally, the U.S. government's role in these global forums has been to assume that what is good for Disney and Rupert Murdoch and General Electric is good for the people of America and the world. It is imperative that the United States' position on crucial global media policy deliberations be based upon broad input from the American people, not upon the wishes of massive campaign contributors.

STRATEGY FOR THE MEDIA REFORM MOVEMENT

It is one thing to chronicle the emergence of interest in media reform and to outline the important policy issues involved, but something else to organize effective political campaigns to achieve the difficult goal of structural media reform. The corporate media lobbies are very strong and politicians are reluctant to tangle with them. Broadcast outlets provide media reform little or no coverage, so it is harder to organize around this issue than an issue where the corporate media do not have an immediate stake in the outcome. These obstacles explain why media reform remained off the political agenda as long as it did, despite the clear role of media in the decline of our political culture.

As recently as 2002, the U.S. media reform movement was comprised of a handful of outstanding but very small shops in Washington, D.C. that tended to focus on a select number of policy issues. There were also a handful of much larger groups, including media-workers unions and the Consumers Union that worked on media policy issues, but did so as a small part of their operations. And there was notable activity at the local level, though it was starving for resources and effectiveness varied. In short, the movement was weak, lacking direction, especially in comparison to its adversaries, and was unknown to 99 percent of the American public.

It was in this environment that we co-founded Free Press in December 2002, along with veteran campaign finance activist Josh Silver. We had a political vision for the media reform movement and we saw Free Press as the vehicle to make it possible for the movement to be politically effective. In our view, Free Press would place emphasis first and foremost on popularizing media policy debates and linking up grassroots concerns with inside-the-beltway deliberations. Our starting point was the Saul Alinsky maxim that the only way to defeat organized money is with organized people. We wanted to have one foot in the present, waging the immediate and often defensive fights, and one foot in the future anticipating what the big fights and proactive possibilities would be in the years to come. After all, this is how the corporate media giants think with their phalanx of lobbyists.

Free Press needed to provide the glue that would draw together the disparate elements of the emerging media reform movement; it had to make the whole greater than the sum of its parts and it had to provide resources and leadership to dramatically increase the number of parts. Free Press would be the one organization that would cover the entire range of media reform issues. We believed that we could have real success in any particular media-policy issue only if we could draw people interested in different but related issues into the fold. So, for example, in the case of media ownership, Free Press, along with the entirety of the media reform movement, worked to build coalitions of musicians concerned about radio concentration, parents concerned about hypercommercialism, and journalists concerned about corporate downsizing in newsrooms. We also knew it was essential to do sustained outreach to other organized constituencies that had a stake in media reform but were inactive in the area. To that end Free Press built the portal www.freepress.net, and it sponsored national conferences in 2003 and 2005 for thousands of media reform activists to come together to discuss strategy and tactics and to find common ground.

Free Press grew dramatically over its first thirty months. As we write this in mid-2005, Free Press has a paid staff of fifteen people conducting a wide range of media policy reform work and public outreach. Free Press has a membership of two hundred thousand people. It is the largest media reform organization in the nation, if not the world, and we would like to believe the growth reflects the strength of our vision and, more important, the quality of work being done by the staff of Free Press. But more than anything it reflects the explosion of interest in this issue. Any lingering doubts about the saliency of media reform as an issue, any suspicions that the media ownership fight of 2003 was a one-hit wonder, were erased in June 2005 when MoveOn received the strongest response in its history to its outreach concerning public broadcasting.

The dramatic emergence of Free Press should not obscure the existence of a much broader and diverse media-reform movement. From independent media centers and groups devoted to media justice to media educators and large membership organizations like Consumers Union and Common Cause the movement is exploding, and Free Press is just a small sliver of the activity, albeit a visible sliver. In fact, our vision of the policy activism branch of the media reform movement is not to have Free Press become an *uber-* group with a series of local chapters. To the contrary, we envision a movement built upon a large number of autonomous local and grassroots organizations, as well as a number of national groups with expertise in specific issues and/or large memberships to draw upon. In the coming years we will see alliances among groups from around the world. Free Press will be *a* leader—not *the* leader—of this movement. The movement has to be heterogeneous and cooperative if it is to ever build up the political muscle to win major victories. This is the process that is beginning to emerge.

The experience of the past three years has left us with two general observations about the strategic possibilities and issues facing the media reform movement. The first is a broad observation on the relationship of the media reform movement to partisan politics, and the second is a narrower assessment on the capacity of media reform to rally popular interest.

We are proud progressives. We wake up every day committed to seeing a world without militarism, social and economic inequality, poverty, political corruption, injustice, and environmental catastrophe. It is this passion for liberty and justice that drives our commitment to participatory democracy and, with that, to media reform. Many people in the media reform movement share our commitment to progressive values, though that hardly makes us a homogeneous group. But there are other routes to joining the media reform movement than via a commitment to progressive politics. This is a lesson we have learned in the past three years, and it holds out tremendous promise for us.

In a very important sense, media reform is a nonpartisan movement. This issue cannot succeed if it is regarded as a fight between one political faction against another political faction to see that one side gets better coverage in the media. It has to be a principled fight for democratic policymaking, with reform proposals that do not necessarily favor one viewpoint over another, but advance democratic values. The media ownership fight in 2003 revealed that many self-described conservatives dislike the idea of media concentration and like the idea of having locally owned media. Subsequent work has established that many conservatives are also appalled at the commercial carpet bombing of childhood in the United States. Indeed, in 2005, research made it clear that a significant percentage of conservatives not only support public broadcasting, they wish to see it expanded and to have commercial influence and political interference reduced.

Besides being philosophically and linguistically accurate to term media reform a nonpartisan movement, it is also strategically and tactically imperative to do so. Not only is there considerable potential for conservative support for specific media reform issues, but it is this prospect that terrifies our opponents, the media giants and their politicians and ideologues. For years our opponents all but ignored us, but by 2005 we were in their sights and they are now returning fire. The last thing our opponents want is an open debate on the issues, because they know their chances in such a debate are not good; they saw how rank-and-file conservatives opposed media consolidation en masse in 2003. To make the media–reform movement illegitimate, to keep us ignored, right-wing groups like Accuracy In Media accuse the media–reform movement of being strictly a left-wing movement dedicated to replacing the Limbaughs and Hannitys with Frankens and Garofalos. This is a preposterous charge, without an iota of evidence. In a mere thirty seconds on his nationally syndicated program in May 2005, Rush Limbaugh dismissed media reformers as "completely insane," "unhinged," and "off their rockers." Of course, he gave his bewildered listeners no context to evaluate what he was talking about. Apologists for big media pursue this course because they know they cannot win an honest debate; we cannot allow them to convert this into a partisan issue.

As in struggles over trade policy and civil liberties, which have also seen complex ideological coalitions develop, the left–right alliance on media reform is a difficult and important relationship that needs cultivating. But while there is some common ground, there are also numerous points of divergence. For example, the media reform movement is opposed to government censorship. So it was in 2005 that the media reform movement almost in toto opposed the law passed by Congress to increase the fines on broadcasters for indecent programming. It was a bill with near unanimous support from conservative politicians and organizations, as well as many moderate Democrats. In our view, the enlightened way to address vulgar fare is to create a structure where it is not a rational thing to produce such content. Since the leading purveyors of vulgarity tend to be the largest media chains with the most desperate pursuit of quick and easy profit, perhaps an ownership policy which favored competition, more nonprofit and community stations, and more local ownership would produce less vulgar fare without empowering government censors.

So this matter of political partisanship is complex. In the current situation, the media system is dominated by massive corporations and commercial values. The political Right has been able to exert considerable influence over news-media content. On this alone, one could see the attraction of some conservatives, or those enthralled with corporate power and commercial values, for the status quo. Likewise, on these grounds alone, one could see why progressives would be alarmed by the media situation in the United States. And that fuels much of the liberal interest in the matter. In 2005, the Bush administration did much to turn this into a partisan issue. As discussed in chapter 3, it engaged in payola punditry and produced fake news to promote its policies. Bush's hand-picked head of the Corporation for Public Broadcasting, Kenneth Tomlinson, went on a secret campaign to remove "liberal bias" from public radio and television and to ensure that the range of journalism and debate on PBS and NPR came as close to his beloved FOX News as possible.

But there is another way to consider this issue. We have never claimed nor do we believe that media reform is a panacea for all major social problems. Simply reforming the media system, and leaving everything else intact, if that were even possible, would not solve all our problems. We often write about how journalism is necessary for meaningful democracy; as Madison warned, self-government will degenerate toward tragedy or farce without a viable media system. But the converse is true as well: Media, especially journalism, require democracy. Without a democratic culture of openness and debate, meaningful journalism cannot occur. If there is not a viable democratic political system and culture, no media reform in the world could produce a healthy journalism. In this sense media reform is al-

ways best understood as one of many core issues that require attention to enhance democracy: reducing economic and social inequality,
eliminating racial and gender bias, expanding and improving access to
education, having open and accountable government, fair and legitimate electoral systems, and so on. In this sense, media reform tends to
be a liberal or progressive movement; it is hardly neutral about how
other core issues are resolved in society.

This explains why at an even deeper level, media reform is of particular interest to liberals, progressives, and those on the broadly defined left. It is not merely that progressives are appalled by the
right-wing tilt of much of the news media or that progressives are dis-
mayed that the causes they are advancing are undermined by the
media, though these are clear factors. It is also that a commitment to
a democratic society must have as a cornerstone a commitment to a
healthy and vibrant press system that draws the citizenry into active
public life. This value is not as common among conservatives, although it is found among principled conservatives. Unfortunately,
those atop today's conservative movement, who are not especially
principled, regard media cynically as simply one more vehicle to manipulate the population.

And practically this means something quite important: Media reform, ultimately, cannot succeed unless there is movement on a
whole range of democratic issues. In the end they rise and fall together. That is why arguably the central factor that will explain the
success of the media reform movement in the coming years will be
how much it is embraced by other progressive movements, activists,
and organizations, and how successful these movements are in their
own right. It is clear in our mind that progressive movements that ignore media reform not only doom media reform, they doom themselves.

This places media reform in a difficult, though by no means impossible, position: to be both nonpartisan and progressive. The way
we have tried to frame the politics of the media-reform movement
since well before the launching of Free Press was to see it as following

in the footsteps of the environmental movement. Our job is not to get caught up in supporting specific politicians or parties; we attempt to educate and work with all parties and clearly work closest with those that are most sympathetic. Our job is simply to make media an issue and to generate massive grassroots pressure on whoever holds office. In 1960, it was rare to hear a politician talk about the environment. By 1972, after exceptional grassroots organizing, no politician or party could afford to ignore the environment. People often forget that the president who signed the most progressive environmental legislation in U.S. history was Richard Nixon. He did so not because he gave a hoot about the environment, but because he feared a negative reaction among voters if he failed to heed popular pressure.

This then is the model for the media reform movement. We need to make media policy a legitimate political issue, an issue that all politicians and parties need to address. We have to remove it from the corrupt proverbial smoke-filled rooms and shine the light of public attention upon it. It is clear that those who benefit from the status quo understand the situation this way; they know their success is directly related to their ability to keep citizens in the dark about their privileged role in determining media policy. During the 2003 media-ownership fight, the Bush administration made protecting the interests of the big media firms one of is highest priorities, but the president and his aides were loathe to mention this in any political campaign. The Bush administration, like the big media corporations, knew that this was a clunker issue for them with the general population. The less said the better.

All of our experience tells us that if there is a fair and open fight, our chances for success are very good.

In 2004 and 2005, the media reform movement has made important headway. Pressure from unions that represent media workers, particularly the Newspaper Guild section of the Communications Workers of America, led the Democratic Party to include a section on media reform in its platform, something not seen for decades. Several Democratic presidential aspirants, including Howard Dean and

Dennis Kucinich, made media reform an issue in their campaigns, as did independent and third-party candidates such as Ralph Nader and Green Party nominee David Cobb. A handful of congressional candidates raised the issue in their campaigns. Most were Democrats or progressive Independents such as Vermont Representative Bernie Sanders. But there are sympathetic Republicans as well, some of whom have stood up to severe pressure from the White House. The growing awareness among honest elected officials and candidates that media must be an issue in our politics—an awareness that mirrors that of millions of Americans—is the most encouraging development of the past several years. Still, our politics have a long way to go before media is the issue it should be. When candidates begin to routinely hear about media from their constituents, when large labor unions, environmental and church groups push the issue as part of their broader agendas, then the battle will have begun to be won. Grassroots heat is what will produce results.

This leads directly to the second strategic conclusion we have reached concerning the capacity of media reform to capture the popular imagination and rally widespread interest and support. The conventional wisdom, pre-2003, was that media reform was a nonstarter with the general population for reasons already discussed. The lesson of the past few years is that once people understand that the current media system is not something natural, like a mountain range, but something determined by policies made in their name, they can and will become engaged. This is not to say that organizing around media reform is easy; the hard work of organizing is still in front of us. Despite its powerful critique of media's relationship to social injustice and racism, the media reform movement is only beginning to make significant headway in communities of color. The vast majority of Americans are still unaware of its existence. But what we know now is that this is not impossible or hopeless organizing. It is more like throwing seeds onto ten-foot-deep Iowa topsoil, than it is like tossing seeds onto a parking lot and praying for a miracle.

Another reason media reform might enjoy popular success is that incremental victories are possible. It is not like campaign finance reform where all the chips are on one number, so to speak. Unless you get publicly funded elections, or some other megareform that leaves no loopholes, it is hard to win in the area of campaign finance reform. Big money will drive a truck through the slightest crack in the reform edifice. Hence, the campaign finance movement has struggled to get traction in the past few years, despite the fact that the 2004 election was the most money-drenched in U.S. history by a wide margin.

Not so with media reform. It is possible to win tangible and discreet victories in the near term. Already, in just two years, the media reform movement has played an integral role in stopping the effort to relax media ownership rules: it has stopped Sinclair Broadcasting from airing blatant propaganda as election news on the public airwaves, it has exposed and stopped the Bush administration and the government from producing fake TV news reports and bribing journalists, and it has organized a firestorm of public outrage to prevent the Bush administration from neutering what remains of public broadcasting. Without the media reform movement, it is possible that one or two of these victories might have still taken place, but the degree of difficulty would have been considerably higher. Political organizing works. And now, for the first time, corporate media lobbyists and the politicians who carry their water must factor in an aroused and energized public as they map their actions.

Nor, even in these corrupt times, are the victories only of a defensive nature. The media reform movement has been instrumental in establishing policies to protect and promote the burgeoning network of community Internet systems. In another example, over the course of 2004 and 2005, scores of new low-power community FM radio stations are being launched, as a result of popular pressure on Congress and the FCC. These stations are going to be on the dial in communities across the nation. People in those communities will see the fruits of their organizing. It will help fuel continued interest in media reform work. Indeed, media reform may well be moving from being a sleeper issue to being a gateway issue that can draw people into politics, especially to progressive politics. The media reform movement highlights the corruption of the political process, the linkage between state and corporate power, and the importance of participatory democracy.

CONCLUSION

We decided to write this book during the course of 2004 as we grew to be more and more appalled by media coverage of the Iraq war and of the presidential election. It was apparent to us then, as it is now, that the wheels had come off of journalism in the United States, that our media system was an abject failure from a democratic perspective, and that our country had entered precisely the zone James Madison warned us against. If the war was tragedy, then the election was farce. It was evident to us that the crisis was severe and the stakes could not be higher.

But, while we were horrified by the day-to-day coverage—or, in many cases, noncoverage—of the war and the election, we did not set out to pen another damning critique of the performance of the mainstream media. Our point with this book, as with all of our work, has been to place the current media crisis in historical context and to locate it on the political map. Our goal ultimately is to encourage active public participation and organizing to change this media system for the better. We believe it is possible to create a system where it is no longer irrational to produce the caliber of journalism and media content a self-governing people require to succeed. And we make this argument with a good deal of optimism for we have seen the dramatic increase in interest in media politics over the past few years.

But we are also realists. It will not be an easy fight to win the battle or even to make genuine progress. The forces of darkness are powerful and they will fight us tooth and nail, as if their very survival rests on the outcome. What gives us confidence in the face of such a fight is the fact that we now have a historic window of opportunity to make media reform an issue in our country's political life. For the next few years—we have no idea exactly how long—we are in one of those rare historical periods where we actually hold the future in our hands, where what we do or do not do can make all the difference. We are reminded of something Noam Chomsky said: "If you act like change for the better is impossible, you guarantee it will be impossible." We have chosen to act like change for the better is possible. We have chosen to believe, as Madison did, that "a people who mean to be their own Governors, must arm themselves with the power knowledge gives." And the way to begin doing so is by forging a media system capable of assuring that that knowledge—and the power to use it—will be the birthright of every American.

SOURCES

Some of the contextual material in the book draws from research we did for our other recent books, in particular McChesney's *The Problem of the Media* and Nichols's *Dick* and *Against the Beast*. Much of the analysis in chapter 3 stands on the foundation provided by Edward S. Herman and Noam Chomsky. We also list below many of the recent books and articles that assisted us directly with this book. The sources for the quotations in the book are almost all listed below by the author's names, or as indicated in the text. Those quotations from the book not listed below came from dozens of interviews we conducted in 2004 and 2005 as we completed research for the book. Much of the material in the book is a result of these interviews and from our personal involvement with media and politics between 2003 and 2005.

Ackerman, Andrew. "War Reporters at ASNE Say Iraq Remains Frightening." *Editor & Publisher*. April 15, 2005.

Ahmed, Nafeez Mosaddeq. The War on Truth: 9/11, Disinformation, and the Anatomy of Terrorism. Northampton, Mass.: Olive Branch Press, 2005.

Alter, Jonathan. "The Left's Mr. Right?" *Newsweek*. August 5, 2003.

Alterman, Eric. "Bush's War on the Press." *The Nation*. May 9, 2005.

———. "Case Closed." *The Nation*. April 25, 2005.

Alvarez, Lizette. "Rights Group Defends Chastising of U.S." *New York Times*. June 4, 2005.

Anderson, Bonnie M. *News Flash*. San Francisco: Jossey Bass, 2004.

Bagdikian, Ben H. *The New Media Monopoly*. Boston: Beacon Press, 2004.

Baker, Russ. "Comparing American and British War Coverage." *AlterNet.org*. April 28, 2003.

———. "Miller's UN Reporting." *The Nation*. April 18, 2005.

———. "Scoops and Truth at the *Times.*" *AlterNet.org*. June 9, 2003.

Barstow, David and Robin Stein. "Under Bush, A New Age of Prepackaged TV News." *New York Times*. March 13, 2005.

Berkowitz, Bill. "Media AWOL on WMD." *TomPaine.com*. January 9, 2004.

Brown, Tina. "Breaking the News, The Becoming It." *Washington Post.* September 23, 2004.

Castro, Max. "Was *Times* Coverage Tainted?" *Miami Herald.* July 1, 2003.

Chancellor, Carl. "Kucinich Says Media Unfairly Bypasses Him as 'Fringe' Candidate." *Knight Ridder* wire service report. November 30, 2003.

Christensen, Christian. "It's Official! 'Iraq Coverage Wasn't Biased.' " *CommonDreams.org.* March 14, 2005.

Chen, Elliot D. *News Incorporated: Corporate Media Ownership and Its Threat to Democracy.* Amherst, N.Y.: Prometheus, 2005.

CNN report on Kerry outburst. "Kerry to speak at college where Cheney delivered critical speech: School president invites Democrat." April 29, 2004.

Cockburn, Alexander. "John the 14 Percent Club! We Won!" *The Nation.* May 30, 2005.

Cohen, Jeff. "Jeff Cohen on the Media and the Election." Speech to the International Labor Communications Association. November 19, 2004.

Coleman, Carole. "President George W Bush - A special edition on the eve of the US leader's visit to Ireland, broadcast live from Washington & Dublin." RTE News, (http://www.rte.ie/news). June 24, 2004.

Conason, Joe. "A Press Coverup." *www.salon.com.* June 17, 2005.

Conyers, John. Letter to Michael Abramowitz, National Editor; Mr. Michael Getler, Ombudsman; Mr. Dana Milbank; The *Washington Post* http://washingtonpost.com. June 17, 2005.

————. "Preserving Democracy: What Went Wrong in Ohio." Status Report of the House Judiciary Committee Democratic Staff. January 5, 2005.

Copps, Michael. "FCC Commissioner Copps: Criticizes Sinclair Corporate Decision to Preempt Local Stations for Political Broadcast." FCC media release. October 22, 2004.

"Counting the Iraqi Dead." *Fair.org.* March 21, 2005.

Cunningham, Brent. "Rethinking Objectivity." *Columbia Journalism Review.* July-August, 2003.

Dean, John. *Worse Than Watergate: The Secret Presidency of George W. Bush.* Little, Brown, 2004.

Digby. "The Blogosphere: Insiders vs. Outsiders." *In These Times.com.* May 9, 2005.

Dreyfuss, Robert. "A Memo And Two Catechisms." *TomPaine.com.* May 23, 2005.

————. "Iraq's Catch-22." *TomPaine.com.* April 19, 2005.

E&P Staff. "Press Routinely Undercounts U.S. Casualties in Iraq." *Editor & Publisher.* November 25, 2004.

————. "Reporter Apologizes for Iraq Coverage." *Editor & Publisher.* March 30, 2004.

Ellis, Rick. "The Surrender of MSNBC." *Allyourtv.com.* February 25, 2003.

Engelhardt, Tom. "Which War Is This Anyway?" *TomDispatch.com.* March 10, 2005.

Entman, Robert M. *Projections of Power: Framing News, Public Opinion, and U.S. Foreign Policy.* Chicago: University of Chicago Press, 2005.

Fabrizio, Tony. "Swift Boat 'controversy' gets Voters' attention and nicks Kerry." Media Release, August 11, 2004.

Fairness & Accuracy in Reporting (FAIR). "ABC Narrows the Field: Did Kucinich's criticism of Koppel influence decision?" December 11, 2003.

Fenton, Tom. *Bad News: The Decline of Reporting, the Business of News, and the Danger to Us All.* New York: HarperCollins, 2005.

Fleischer, Ari. White House press briefing, September 26, 2001.

Friel, Howard and Richard A. Falk. *The Record of the Paper: How the* New York Times *Misreports U.S. Foreign Policy.* New York: Verso, 2004.

Fritz, Ben, Bryan Keefer, and Brendan Nyhan. *All the President's Spin: George W. Bush, the Media, and the Truth.* New York: Touchstone, 2004.

Gandy, Kim. "Speech to National Conference for Media Reform." St. Louis, Mo., May 14, 2005.

"Garrett of 'Newsday' Rips Tribune Co. 'Greed' in Exit Memo." *Editor & Publisher.* March 1, 2005.

Gillmor, Dan. *We the Media: Grassroots Journalism by the People, for the People.* Sebastopol, Calif.: O'Reilly, 2004.

Goldsborough, James. "On the Iraq War, the Press Failed the Public." *San Diego Union-Tribune.* April 19, 2004.

Guider, Elizabeth. "Media Conglomerates Muzzling Dissent." *Variety.com.* September 5, 2004.

Hart, Peter. "The Great Emancipator: Media credit Bush for 'Democratization' of the Mideast." *Extra!.* May/June 2005.

———. "Target Dean." *Extra!,* http://www.fair.org/index.php? page-1176. March/April 2004.

Hedges, Chris. "The Press and the Myths of War." *The Nation.* April 21, 2003.

Herbert, Bob. "The Agony of War." *New York Times.* April 25, 2005.

Herman, Edward S. and Noam Chomsky. *Manufacturing Consent: The Political Economy of the Mass Media.* New York: Pantheon, 1989.

Hersh, Seymour. "The Unknown Unknowns of the Abu Ghraib Scandal." *The Guardian.* May 21, 2005.

Hersh, Seymour and Jonathan Schell. "Two Acclaimed Journalists Discuss Press and Politics." *The Dart Center for Journalism and Trauma.* November 10, 2004.

Hewitt, Hugh. *Blog: Understanding the Information Reformation That's Changing Your World.* Nashville, Tenn.: Thomas Nelson, 2005.

"Interview with Newt Gingrich." *Broadcasting & Cable,* March 20, 1995.

"Iraq, Then and Now." *Washington Post.* June 15, 2005.

Ivins, Molly, with Lou Dubose. *Shrub: The Short but Happy Political Life of George W. Bush.* New York: Random House, 2000.

Jamieson, Kathleen Hall. University of Pennsylvania's National Annenberg Election Survey. Annenberg Public Policy Center, 2004.

Keene Sentinel. "Keene Sentinel Editorial: Howard Dean in the N.H. Primary." January 18, 2004.

Klein, Naomi. "Brand USA is in Trouble, So Take a Lesson from Big Mac." *The Guardian.* March 14, 2005.

Krugman, Paul. "America Held Hostage." *New York Times.* July 1, 2005.

――――. "The War President." *New York Times.* June 24, 2005.

Kucinich, Dennis. "Kucinich Releases Media Reform Plan." Campaign press release. December 13, 2003.

Kurtz, Howard. "Paint by Numbers: How Repeated Reportage Colors Perceptions" (Media Notes). *Washington Post.* July 12, 2004.

――――. "John Kerry, Media Critic" (Media Notes). *Washington Post.* March 15, 2005.

Lessin, Nancy and Gordon Clark. "Stop Hiding the Toll of War." *CommonDreams.org.* March 5, 2004.

Lewis, Charles. "The Lessons of Watergate." The Center for Public Integrity. December 1, 2004.

Lindorff, David. "The Emperor's New Hump." *Extra!,* http://www.fair .org/index.php?page=2012. January/February 2005.

"Local Stations Are Big Winners in Campaign 2004." *The Political Standard.* Vol. 7, No. 4. December 2004.

Madison, James. *Advice to My Country.* Charlottesville, Va.: University Press of Virginia, 1997.

Massing, Michael. "Iraq, the Press and the Election." *New York Review of Books.* December 16, 2004.

――――. "Now They Tell Us." *New York Review of Books.* February 26, 2004.

Matthews, Chris. "Howard Dean on his Remarks on Terror Warning." MSNBC, *Hardball* transcript. December 1, 2003.

Mazzetti, Mark. "PR Meets Psy-Ops in War on Terror." *Los Angeles Times.* December 1, 2004.

McChesney, Robert W. *The Problem of the Media.* New York: Monthly Review Press, 2004.

McChesney, Robert W. and Ben Scott. *Our Unfree Press.* New York: The New Press, 2004.

McChesney, Robert W., Russell Newman and Ben Scott. *The Future of Media.* New York: Seven Stories Press, 2005.

Media for Democracy 2004. "Horse Race Tramples the Issues." www.mfd2004.us. January 30, 2004.

Mercier, Rick. "Why the Media Owe You an Apology on Iraq." *The Free Lance-Star* (Fredericksburg, Va.). March 28, 2004.

Mermin, Jonathan. *Debating War and Peace: Media Coverage of U.S. Intervention in the Post-Vietnam Era.* Princeton: Princeton University Press, 1999.

———. "The Media's Independence Problem." *World Policy Journal.* Vol. 21, No. 3. Fall 2004.

Merritt, Davis. *Knightfall: Knight Ridder and How the Erosion of Newspaper Journalism Is Putting Democracy at Risk.* New York: Amacom, 2005.

Milibank, Dana. "Democrats Play House To Rally Against the War." *The Washington Post.* June 17, 2005

Mindich, David T. Z. *Tuned Out: Why Americans Under 40 Don't Follow the News.* New York: Oxford University Press, 2005.

Moeller, Susan. "How the Media Blew the Iraq Story." *Newsday.* April 21, 2004.

Moline, Matt. "MSNBC's Banfield: Media Filtered Realities of War." *Topeka Capital-Journal.* April 26, 2003.

Montopoli, Brian, with Thomas Lang and Zachary Roth. "Ambush!" CJR Daily, http://www.cjrdaily.org/archives/000851.asp. August 25, 2004.

Moyers, Bill. "Speech to National Conference for Media Reform." St. Louis, Mo., www.freepress.net. May 15, 2005.

Navasky, Victor. *A Matter of Opinion.* New York: Farrar, Straus and Giroux, 2005.

Nichols, John. *Against the Beast: An Anti-Imperialist Reader.* New York: Nation Books, 2004.

———. *Dick: The Man Who Is President.* New York: The New Press, 2004.

———. "Stenographers to Power." *CommonDreams.org.* November 23, 2004.

O'Carroll, Lisa. "Murdoch brings in Bush adviser." *The Guardian.* March 19, 2004.

Olson, Erin. "Why Does 'NY Times' Call Casualty Count from April Fallujah Battle 'Inflated' or 'Unconfirmed'?" *Editor & Publisher.* November 23, 2004.

O'Reilly, Bill. "Transcript: Bush Talks to O'Reilly." FOX News Channel Interview Archive. September 28, 2004.

Rampton, Sheldon and John Stauber. *Weapons of Mass Deception: The Uses of Propaganda in Bush's War on Iraq.* Jeremy P. Tarcher, 2003.

Rangwala, Glen. "Claims in Secretary of State Colin Powell's UN Presentation Concerning Iraq, 5th Feb 2003." *http://middleeastreference.org.uk/powell030205.html.*

Rendall, Steve and Tara Broughel. "Amplifying Officials, Squelching Dissent: FAIR Study Finds Democracy Poorly Served by War Coverage." *Extra!.* May/June, 2003, *http://www.fair.org/extra/0305/warstudy.html.*

Ritter, Scott. "Is Iraq a True Threat to the US?" *Boston Globe.* July 20, 2002.

Roberts, Gene, Thomas Kunkel and Charles Layton, eds. *Leaving Readers Behind: The Age of Corporate Newspapering.* Fayetteville: University of Arkansas Press, 2001.

Roberts, L. et al. "Mortality Before and After the 2003 Invasion of Iraq: Cluster Sample Survey." *The Lancet.* 364(9448), pp. 1857–64.

Roberts, Paul Craig. "Bush's Ruinouis Empire." CounterPunch website. June 27, 2005.

Roos, Jonathan. "Dean Flag Comments Offensive, Rivals Say." *Des Moines Register.* November 2, 2003.

Rosenfeld, Steven. "Media Culpa." *AlterNet.org.* September 10, 2004.

Rutherford, Paul. *Weapons of Mass Persuasion: Marketing the War Against Iraq.* Toronto: University of Toronto Press, 2004.

Rutenberg, Jim. "Cable's War Coverage Suggests a New 'Fox Effect' on Television." *New York Times.* April 16, 2003.

Sack, Kevin. "Gingrich Attacks the Media as Out of Touch." *New York Times,* April 23, 1997.

Salutin, Rick. "The Media Disappeared Howard Dean." *Toronto Star.* February 6, 2004.

Saunders, Sakura, with Ben Clarke. "Media corporations give millions, receive billions." *CorpWatch.org.* August 25, 2004.

Schechter, Danny. *Embedded: Weapons of Mass Deception: How the Media Failed to Cover the War on Iraq.* Prometheus, 2003.

———. "From Florida to Fallujah: What the News Coverage Covers Up." *MediaChannel.org.* November 9, 2004.

———. "The Iraq Scandals: Media Failures Are Next." *MediaChannel.org.* July 19, 2004.

———. "Is Our Media Covering Its Errors or Covering Them Up?" *Common Dreams.org.* August 16, 2004.

Seuss, Dr. *The 500 Hats of Bartholomew Cubbins.* New York: Random House, 1938.

Shaw, David. "Is Bush really implementing a full-court press on media?" *Los Angeles Times.* March 13, 2005.

Snow, Nancy. *Information War: American Propaganda, Free Speech, and Opinion Control Since 9/11.* New York: Seven Stories, 2004.

Solomon, Norman.. "A Voluntary Tic in Media Coverage of Iraq." *Common Dreams.org.* November 18, 2004.

———. "Linking the Occupation of Iraq with the 'War on Terrorism'." *AlterNet.org.* November 21, 2003.

———. "The P.U.-litzer Prizes for 2004." *AlterNet.org.* December 10, 2004.

———. "War and Forgetfulness—A Bloody Media Game." Syndicated newspaper column. August 1, 2002.

——— *War Made Easy: How Presidents and Pundits Keep Spinning Us to Death.* Hoboken, N.J.: John Wiley & Sons, 2005.

Steele, Jonathan. "Don't Be Fooled by the Spin on Iraq." *The Guardian.* April 13, 2005.

Stepp, Carl Sessions. "Journalism without Profit Margins." *American Journalism Review.* October-November 2004.

Strupp, Joe. "Annual 'State of Media' Study Finds Newspapers Slipping." *Editor & Publisher.* March 13, 2005.

SOURCES

Sussman, Peter Y. "Media Loses the War." *AlterNet.org.* May 20, 2003.

Thomas, Helen. "Pentagon Manages War Coverage By Limiting Coffin Pictures." Syndicated column run by Hearst Newspapers. October 30, 2003.

Trippi, Joe. *The Revolution Will Not Be Televised.* New York: HarperCollins, 2004.

Tumulty, Karen. "The Dean Factor." *Time.* August 3, 2003.

"TV News Largely Ignores Local Political Campaigns, New Lear Center Study Finds." *The Political Standard.* Vol. 8, No. 1. March 2005.

Ullman, Harlan and James Wade, Jr. *Shock and Awe: Achieving Rapid Dominance.* Philadelphia: Pavilion Press, no date.

Wasserman, Edward. "Cowardice in the Newsrooms." *Miami Herald.* September 6, 2004.

Weisbrot, Mark. "When the Media Fails." *CommonDreams.org.* May 7, 2003.

Western, Jon. *Selling Intervention & War: The Presidency, the Media, and the American Public.* Baltimore: The Johns Hopkins University Press, 2005.

Wolcott, James. *Attack Poodles and Other Media Mutants.* New York: Miramax Books, 2004.

Woodward, Bob. *Plan of Attack.* New York: Simon & Schuster, 2004.

Zerbisias, Antonia. "The Press Self-muzzled Its Coverage of Iraq War." *Toronto Star.* September 16, 2003.

———. "Tide is Changing in US Coverage of War in Iraq." *Toronto Star.* May 18, 2004.

Zoroya, Gregg. "Return of U.S. War Dead Kept Solemn, Secret." *USA Today.* December 31, 2003.

ACKNOWLEDGMENTS

In the days before the 2004 presidential election, the notion for this book began to develop. It could not have come at a worse time. Both of us were in the thick of other projects, including planning for the second National Conference on Media Reform. It is a testament to the media reform movement, particularly Josh Silver and everyone else at Free Press, that everyone seemed to accept the challenges that researching and writing a new book would impose on our schedules. Andy Hsiao, André Schiffrin, Colin Robinson, Diane Wachtell, and the rest of the team at The New Press embraced the idea from the start and provided crucial support and understanding as deadlines were stretched to accommodate what remained an evolving text right up to the moment of publication. Everyone at the Institute of Communications Research at the University of Illinois at Urbana-Champaign, where Bob teaches, and at *The Nation* and the *Capital Times,* the publications for which John writes, provided a generous mix of tolerance and encouragement. Victor Pickard provided crucial research assistance for chapter 3; without his labor the chapter could not have been written. Eric Magnuson, of *The Nation,* provided research assistance for chapters 4 and 5. The magnificent Jeff Cohen carefully read and edited early drafts of chapters 2, 3, and 6. And special thanks to Dan Perkins for letting us use several of his terrific Tom Tomorrow cartoons. Finally, our families—Aunt Carolyn Fry and Mary Bottari and Whitman Bottari Nichols for John; Inger Stole and Amy & Lucy McChesney for Bob—supported our lunacy more than we deserved, and they kept us within range of sanity.

This book is dedicated to our friends Paul and Sheila Wellstone. When we first went to Capitol Hill looking for members of Congress who might be willing to take on big media, only one senator immediately understood what the fight was about—and the necessity of joining it. That was Paul who wrote the introduction for our first book. At the same time, Sheila, who had spent so many years working on issues of violence against women, helped us to understand the totality of the damage that irresponsible media do in America. We cherish their memory, and we recognize that, when the fight for media reform is finally won, it will be the end of a journey that was begun with two of the finest public servants this nation has ever produced at our side.